Unshakeable

To Live a Life with Strength, Focus, and Heart

Brad C. Wenneberg

Unshakeable

To Live a Life with Strength, Focus, and Heart

ISBN (Paperback): 978-1-969826-24-5
ISBN (Hardcover): 978-1-969826-25-2
ISBN (E-Book): 978-1-969826-26-9

First Edition

Dedication

To my wife, Bonnie —

For over fifty years, you have been my partner in every battle and blessing.

You've walked with me through the storms, lifted me when I couldn't stand, and celebrated every hard-earned victory. You've believed in me when I doubted myself, reminded me of who I was when I forgot, and stood by me when others walked away. We have built dreams together, faced fears together, and found laughter in the middle of tears.

This book, like my life, exists because of your faith, your love, and your unshakeable spirit.
You are my greatest gift, my truest friend,
and my forever partner on this incredible journey.

I love and appreciate you with all my heart.

Foreword

by Caleb Beller, Sensei - American Martial Arts Academy
Student, Friend, 5th Degree Black Belt

Thirty-three years ago, I stepped into Shihan Brad Wenneberg's dojo as a young, uncertain soul searching for direction. I found a mentor, a guide, and a friend whose belief in me changed my life. Shihan didn't just teach me to kick or punch; he taught me to stand tall, show up, and live with purpose.

I was the second student when AMAA opened its doors, and the first student of AMAA to earn the title of Sensei at American Martial Arts Academy. I owe much of my life's work to Shihan Brad. His mantra— "to show up with heart"—helped shape me as a leader, pastor, husband, and father. In *Unshakeable*, the powerful follow-up to his first book, *Unleash Your Inner Warrior*, he distills a lifetime of wisdom into a testament to building not just martial artists, but better humans.

I carry lessons forged in countless hours training and living alongside him. Together, we built American Martial Arts Academy into one of the most successful schools in our country, with a journey of heart as much as hard work. His philosophy was never about trophies but about showing up through pain, doubt, and life's challenges with integrity, resilience, and even a touch of magic to spark joy.

Unshakeable isn't a karate manual. It's an inspiring and insightful journey, as well as a reflection on legacy, family, and the courage to evolve. Shihan shares his battles with illnesses, his shift from the center of the mat to guiding light, and his love for his family and students with vulnerability and humor. His words remind us that legacy is about the lives we touch and the moments we choose to show up.

As you read, you'll hear the voice of a warrior, storyteller, and friend. You'll feel the weight of his worn black belt and the warmth of his belief in second chances. For me, and countless others, Shihan has been the steady hand in shaky times, the heartbeat of a thriving community. This book is his *bow*—not a final one, but a powerful call to tie our belts, step onto Life's mat, and show up with our whole hearts. *Shihan Brad changed my life; this book will change yours.*

Sensei Caleb Beller
Senior Pastor, Calvary Chapel Fullerton
Husband, Father of Four, Missionary, Teacher, Police Chaplain

Introduction - When Life Hits Back

"A storm doesn't make you... it reveals you."
- James Lane Allen

During and after I wrote my first book (*Unleash Your Inner Warrior*), I felt as if my life was in order and all was just right. I wasn't worried or stressed...all was great and met all of my expectations!
You know what they say—"You can make God laugh just by telling Him your plans."

Soon after the release of that book, I got a call from my doctor. He told me I needed to come in as soon as I could. I arrived in a panic. What was going on? This wasn't part of my "plan."

My doctor explained that there was a problem with my prostate and we needed to take immediate action. We quickly made an appointment with a top prostate cancer surgeon at City of Hope.

The night before my appointment, I was sitting in an AA meeting in intense fear, wondering "Why me?" I abruptly stood up and left the meeting. I drove around asking myself, "What now?" My life was going as planned—and now this?

I started thinking about solutions instead of the problem. Maybe I should drink... nah, that would only make it worse. Running away, ignoring it, or wallowing in self-pity weren't real solutions either.

So I followed my own advice—the same principles I wrote about in my first book. I returned to the meeting. I refused to focus on my challenge. Instead, I helped a newcomer. Afterward, we went for coffee and pie and talked for hours. That gentleman is still sober to this day.

After all the tests were done, my wife and I sat facing the doctor. From behind his small desk, he said, "You have prostate cancer, and it's very close to the bone." He suggested immediate surgery.

At that moment, everything got quiet in my head. Time froze. Disbelief and fear set in. My mind raced to the worst-case scenario: How long do I have to live?

But my wife stayed calm. She asked, "What's our next step?" That snapped me out of my spiral. I remembered: I can choose to live in the problem, or I can find peace by choosing to live in the solution.

We acted. I had the surgery, and it was successful. I thought I'd just return to life as it was... nope. There was more to come.

After a year of recovery, I had to face a new reality, especially around intimacy with my wife. I still functioned, but it was very different. I was no longer the man I once was, and my ego went wild. I didn't feel like a man anymore.

Redefining intimacy was one of the hardest emotional struggles I've ever faced. But over time, I gained a new understanding. It wasn't just about physical activity – it was about connection, closeness, and love. My wife simply said, "We will adapt. We always have."

I still struggle at times with sadness for what I lost. But I've also found a deeper appreciation for what I've gained - a renewed understanding of love, and the fact that I am still alive and cancer-free.

When I start to drift back into fear or discouragement, my wife reminds me, “Read your own book.”

This isn’t just my story—it’s your invitation.

If you’ve ever felt stuck, lost, unworthy, or uncertain, the chapters ahead will offer tools, truths, and training to help you stand-up—stronger, clearer, and unshakeable.

So... what’s in it for you?

You’ll find more than motivation here—you’ll find principles that work. This book isn’t about theory or fluff. It’s about real life. It’s about rising from rejection, finding purpose after failure, leading with love, and living with integrity—even when life hits back – even when life shakes you to your core.

Each chapter is rooted in decades of experience from the dojo, the streets, the boardroom, and the heart. These are not lessons from a pedestal—they’re hard-earned truths from the mat.

You’ll laugh. You’ll reflect. You might even cry. But most of all, you’ll be reminded that you are not alone—and you are not without power.

So whether you’re rebuilding something broken, refining what’s already strong, or just ready for your next level... welcome.

Let’s walk this path together—one step, one stance, one story at a time.

"The oak fought the wind and was broken.
The willow bent when it must, and survived."
— Robert Jordan

Testimonials

Jesse Bernal

Martial Arts School Owner (Colorado), Sr. Black Belt

"I met Shihan Wenneberg in 2007. Luck or kismet—it was supposed to happen, because it did. At first, I misunderstood the man behind the title. But years later, I read his first book *(Unleash Your Inner Warrior*) and joined his coaching group—and my life and business changed forever.

Brad's influence is quiet but intentional. He helped our family, not with grand gestures, but with small, purposeful acts of service. Today, he is one of my most trusted mentors. His wisdom, presence, and servant leadership are real—and rare.

As Brad says: *'The past is an indicator of the future.'* I look forward to this book making the same impact his life has made on me."

Deidre King

Black Belt, Instructor, Mother

"I came to the dojo as a perfectionist mom just trying to raise her kids right. I left as a Black Belt who finally learned to give herself grace.

Shihan once asked me a simple question— 'Why?'—and it cracked open years of emotional armor I didn't know I was wearing. Karate didn't just strengthen my body—it began a healing I didn't even know I needed.

When I teach now, I bring that empathy into every lesson. Shihan didn't just change my *kata*. He helped me rewrite my story."

Danny Bower

Black Belt, Student, Sponsee

"Brad Wenneberg is my Shihan, my sponsor, my mentor, and my friend. One day, he invited me into his karate academy and challenged me to 'give him a year.'

I stepped into that dojo with white hair, a white gi, and a white belt. Today, I'm a Black Belt with confidence and focus.

Shihan's true passion isn't just martial arts—it's mentoring people like me. His books reflect the principles he lives in every day. This one is no exception. It's not just a book—it's a blueprint."

Adrian Corfar

Black Belt, Instructor, Leader

"I started training with Shihan when I was six, until I was about twelve. I had learning challenges, physical disabilities, and didn't know where I fit in the world.

Years later, I came back—and Shihan welcomed me like family.

He saw potential I didn't. He invited me into his Business College, mentored me, and helped me leave a minimum wage job for something meaningful.

Today, I'm a Black Belt, instructor, and proud to serve others. We laugh, train hard, and always show respect.

Shihan is 'the bomb'. He changed my life—and I'll never stop being grateful."

Grandmaster Scott Southwick

Founder, Southwick Black Belt Academy (Idaho)

"Shihan Brad gave our family clarity in the chaos. His mentorship helped us grow our business by over 400% and, more importantly, restore peace in our home.

"Few people have impacted my life more deeply than Shihan Brad Wenneberg. At a time when my family and I were overwhelmed—burnout pressing in from all sides—his mentorship offered us something priceless: **clarity**. And with clarity came **relief**. It quieted the chaos, cut through the noise, and gave us space to breathe.

Over five years, our business grew by more than **400%**, but what truly changed was the way we lived. Part-time roles became meaningful careers. Our operations became stronger and more ethical, allowing us to serve our community more effectively.

Most profoundly, the tension in our home eased. With my wife and children by my side on this journey, I watched them grow — not just as professionals, but as people. Shihan didn't just teach us how to run a business; **he showed us how to live with purpose.**

His influence is felt in our decisions, our relationships, and our peace. The clarity he gave us has become the **foundation we stand on — and the legacy we'll carry forward.**"

Karly Feenstra

Student, Sr. Black Belt, Instructor

"*Unshakeable* isn't just a collection of stories. It's not just another self-help book—it's a living, breathing reflection of the man behind the words. This book is a guide to living a life of ambition, integrity, and deep purpose. Every lesson is rooted in real-world experience, not theory. There's no fluff here, no recycled advice—only truth from someone who lives what he teaches.
Whether you're a business owner, a leader, a coach, a parent, or simply someone hungry to grow, *Unshakeable* will challenge your mindset and provide a rock-solid foundation for personal growth. The wisdom in these pages goes beyond martial arts—it's about becoming the strongest, most authentic version of yourself, and using your gifts to serve others and live with purpose."

Thomas Barbarick

Student, Friend, Sr. Black Belt, Retired Navy, Boeing Mgr/Engineer, Fellow Traveler

"I have known Shihan Brad Wenneberg for over 20 years. It has been a fantastic journey of ups and downs. He has been a mentor, coach, teacher, and along the way, a close friend and confidant.

Shihan has made me a better person, and my wife and two adult children have all reaped the benefits of his many years of enriching lives through the martial arts.

When we say that "building and enriching lives through the martial arts" is our mission, with Shihan it's not just a slogan — it's a way of life he truly embodies.

Confidence. Self-respect. Integrity. Perseverance. These are not just buzzwords in his world — they are the pillars he lives by and teaches.

As in martial arts, so in life: Shihan always stresses the basics. Whether running a business, attending school, or building a marriage, success begins with a strong foundation in the fundamentals.

Over the years, I've seen that Shihan speaks from the heart with a passion for people's betterment. He sees the good and the potential in others and has a rare ability to bring out their best. This is true leadership, and Shihan shares it willingly.

He is there when needed — to pick up the pieces, to encourage, to celebrate, or simply to listen. We've shared many stories over the years, some funny, some deeply moving, all without judgment and always with encouragement.

His stories are uplifting and inspiring, offered with the anticipation of positive results. Shihan takes the high road, leads with conviction, and stands as a leader among leaders.

Those who train with him quickly discover that his teaching is about far more than blocks, strikes, and kicks — it's about building the best person you can be. As the ethos at the dojo says:

'Whether you're eight or eighty, Shihan builds strong character and a strong spirit of service.'"

"We cannot live better than in seeking to become better."
- Socrates

Lisa Barbarick
Friend, AMAA Supporter, wife and mother of Black Belts

"Walking into the dojo has always felt like stepping into a space of respect and calm. I've always felt welcome and safe — proud to watch my son and husband train. Shihan Wenneberg's Instructor College became the place where I learned to prioritize my goals and choices. Through Shihan's heartfelt stories, I discovered I could refine my expectations, surround myself with people who bring me joy, and remember that it is never too late to grow. Over more than 20 years, I have grown under Shihan's guidance and friendship."

Captain Ed
Friend, Retired Fire Captain

"I met Brad twenty-five years ago at my very first AA meeting. I was a fire captain, he was a retired police officer, and right away we connected. For the last two and a half decades, we've had dinner and gone to meetings together every Thursday night. In that time, Brad has been more than a friend - he's been a mentor, a brother, and a fellow traveler on this journey of recovery and life.

I read his first book (*Unleash Your Inner Warrior*) and loved it, and I've been fortunate to read a few early chapters of *Unshakeable*.

It's powerful, honest, and true to whom Brad is. He lives what he writes. He's helped countless people - myself included - and I know this book will do the same for anyone who reads it."

FR. Bob Gray

Shihan of Goju Kenkyu and Goju Ryu (San Jose, CA), Friend, Mentor

"I've been privileged to know Brad for more than three decades. His ability to endure, to grow, and to be changed for the better by life's experiences is one of his greatest attributes. Over the years, I've seen many people try to cover their mistakes by calling their darkness 'light.' Brad has never done that. Instead, he grows — not in spite of his trials and mistakes, but because of them. His life is a path of honest progress and transformation.

In this book, Brad shares true gems of wisdom. Wisdom, after all, is the distilled voice of lessons learned through painful moments. You'll find that here. You'll see glimpses of his family, his dojo, his career, and even his humor. But through it all, you'll see the same man: a warrior on the path. By reading this book, you'll be invited to discover, as Brad has, that all of life is a gift. Enjoy. Grow. And keep walking on the sunny side of the street."

Nikhil & Megan Joshi
Students, Sr. Black Belts, Martial Arts Academy Owners

"We've known Shihan Brad Wenneberg for most of our lives, and we can say with complete confidence: he doesn't just talk about leadership, personal growth, and integrity—he lives it.

In a world where many people write books and talk a good game, Shihan Wenneberg stands apart. His actions, transparency, and consistency speak volumes—whether it's in the dojo, in business, in marriage, or in parenting.

This book isn't just filled with ideas. It's filled with wisdom born from experience. If you're willing to be teachable, it will challenge you, inspire you, and truly change your life."

Unshakeable - To Live a Life with Strength, Focus, and Heart

Chapters

Prologue

I was dying. That's how this story begins.

The year was 1978. I was twenty-five years old, desperate and full of shame, lying sleepless on a warm spring night at 3 a.m. I reached to my right, opened the drawer of my nightstand, pulled out my police service revolver—a .357 Magnum—placed the muzzle to my right temple, and pulled the trigger.

During my five years as a police officer, I had never once questioned the reliability of that firearm. But that night, something didn't happen—and I came to realize that my wife, Bonnie, had quietly saved my life.

She awkwardly and instinctively reached out, grabbing the revolver just as I was about to pull the trigger. The next thing I remember was waking up in a hospital bed, strapped down. Bonnie later told me she had unloaded the gun before going to sleep. She had never touched my service weapon before—but she'd had a gut feeling that something was terribly wrong.

I screamed. I tugged at the restraints. I cried and pleaded with anyone who would listen, begging to be released so I could finish what I'd started. But as the hours passed, my rage faded into exhaustion, and exhaustion gave way to something else—a deeper cry, a plea not for death, but for help.
Alone and staring at the ceiling, I began to bargain with the silence. I wanted someone, anyone, to rescue me or give me the magic answer to make the pain go away. Then, in that stillness, I felt a calm wash over me. And although I was alone, I heard a

voice—not with my ears, but deep in my soul. It said, "Remember when you were six years old—passionate, determined, and full of life? You made a promise then: to be happy, to be successful. It's time to honor that promise."

That next morning, I told the nurse she could untie the restraints. I had made a decision—I was done fighting to die. I had chosen to live.

From that moment on, I was determined to never again live my life as a drunk. I knew in my bones that nothing—not alcohol, not shame, not fear—could stand in the way of my dreams. I had a mission, a purpose, and a vision of the man I could become.

I began rebuilding, starting with the fellowship of Alcoholics Anonymous and getting myself immersed in recovery. I pursued a new career in the insurance business and spent a successful decade there, becoming a Million Dollar Round Table member. It was a complete turnaround from the man I had been. And yet, while I found success, something deeper began stirring within me.

I started teaching karate at a local health club. The moment I stepped onto the mat, something clicked. I didn't just enjoy it—I loved it. I was changing from the inside out. The spark had been lit again.

By 1992, I was still happily married to Bonnie. We had two incredible children, Sheri and Jason. Even as my insurance career was thriving, I felt called to a greater vision—one that aligned more fully with my passion and purpose. That summer, I made the bold decision to open my own karate school. My dream: to build the finest teaching institution in the world.

With my family's unwavering support, I opened the American Martial Arts Academy in August 1992. Since then, I've learned through trial and error, through mentorship and perseverance, through determination and cooperation, how to achieve success—emotionally, spiritually, and financially.

I've helped thousands of students grow stronger, not just in body, but in mind and spirit. In the process, I've become someone I can be proud of: a sober man, a husband, a father, a friend, a teacher, a warrior.

This book isn't about theory—it's about what works. What you hold in your hands is the result of decades spent in the arena, rising from rock bottom to build a life rooted in purpose, service, and discipline.

Unshakeable is more than a title—it's a declaration. It's about building a foundation so strong that no storm can knock you out. It's about applying Black Belt principles to everyday life—whether you're in recovery, rebuilding, or simply ready to live with greater clarity and courage.

This book is a roadmap for becoming unshakeable in a shaky world.

If you're tired of white-knuckling life... if you're ready to stop settling and start rising... if you're willing to do the work—then let's walk this path together.

You've got a warrior within you. It's time to wake up that warrior.

Let's get to work.

"Out of suffering have emerged the strongest souls;
the most massive characters are seared with scars."
- Kahlil Gibran

Chapter 1 - The Black Belt Mindset

"The mind is everything.
What you think, you become."
- Buddha

There's a saying in martial arts: *"Where the head goes, the body follows."*
That's not just about balance in a stance — it's a life truth.
The Black Belt Mindset is about training the most powerful weapon we will ever carry: our thinking. While some chase belts or titles, we pursue something deeper — mastery of the mind. **It's one of the Black Belt Basics that makes us Unshakeable, on and off the mat.**

The First Battle is Always Internal

Before we break a board or win a tournament, we must conquer what's inside us:
Fear. Doubt. Ego. Insecurity.

These are the invisible opponents every warrior faces. And the good news? We can train for those fights, too. **Each time we do, we plant our feet a little deeper in the Unshakeable stance — the place where life's hits can't knock us down.**

Just like physical techniques, our mindset can be drilled, refined, and elevated. It starts with awareness — what we think, we become.

If we feed fear, it grows.
If we dwell on resentment, it festers.
If we speak words of defeat, we program ourselves to lose.

But if we speak truth, focus on growth, and act with courage — no matter how small the steps — we're living the Black Belt life, and on our way to becoming Unshakeable.

The Moment That Changed Me

One day in class, a young student froze mid-*kata*. Tears welled in his eyes. He looked at me, shaking his head like he'd failed. I knelt beside him, looked him straight in the eye, and whispered:

A Black Belt isn't someone who never messes up.
A Black Belt is someone who keeps going.

He took a breath... and finished. Wobbly, imperfect, but brave.

I will never forget that. That moment wasn't about his *kata*. It was about his mind.

The Power of Focus

There's a lot of noise in the world — distractions, drama, doubt.

But the mind of a Black Belt cuts through that.

We train ourselves to breathe before we act, listen before we react, and respond with purpose. That takes mental discipline.

Focus isn't just for tournaments - it's for life:

- In arguments with loved ones.

- In business decisions.
- In sobriety and recovery.
- In the middle of storms — both literal and emotional.

Focus is the superpower of the warrior. And it's forged through repetition.

The Archer and the Target (Japanese Legend)

A young samurai wanted to become the best archer in the land. He practiced every day, hitting the target from great distances.

One day, he visited an old master known for his unmatched skill. The master watched the young man hit the bullseye repeatedly, then said, *"You are skilled with the bow, but you are not yet an archer."*

Confused, the young samurai asked why. The master blindfolded himself, drew the bow, and still hit the target.

He explained, *"When you can see the target without your eyes, hear it without your ears, and strike without thought — then you will have the mind of a true archer."*

Lesson: The Black Belt Mindset isn't just about skill — it's about clarity, calm under pressure, and unity of mind and action.

From Law Enforcement to Leadership

In my law enforcement career, I was trained to stay calm under fire. But it was in the dojo — teaching kids, mentoring teens, encouraging nervous parents — that I learned how much deeper mindset training truly goes.

One night, after a long day, I wanted to snap at a disrespectful student. However, I remembered what I often say to others:

We can't control the first thought — but we can choose the second.
That's where the shift happens.

The Samurai and the Peach Pit

An arrogant young samurai once challenged a great master.

He bowed with arrogance and said, *"I've come to defeat you. Prepare yourself."*

The old master didn't flinch. He said calmly, *"Come back when you've cleaned the peach pit out of your heart."*

Confused, the young warrior asked, *"What peach pit?"*

The master replied, *"The one of pride, ego, and fear. A true warrior must face that first."*

The Mental Dojo

Our real training ground isn't just on the mats — it's in our thoughts.

- When we're tired and want to quit, that's the test.
- When someone offends us and we breathe instead of biting back, that's the test.

- When we're facing addiction, fear, financial stress, or heartache — and we still show up — that's the test.

And every time we pass those tests, even in small ways, we strengthen the muscle of the mind.

Unshakeable Reminder –

Train our minds like we train our bodies — with discipline, intention, and purpose.
A true Black Belt isn't forged in the body. It's forged in the mind.

Don't just wear the belt - be the mindset - **because the Unshakeable life begins in the mind - where every victory is first won.**

"Think like a warrior. Be a student. Act like a Black Belt."
- Brad Wenneberg, Shihan

Chapter 2 - Unshakeable Begins With Integrity

"A Black Belt is just a White Belt who showed up like it mattered—every day."

- Brad Wenneberg, Shihan

Before I ever put on a *gi*, before I bowed in for the first time, I was already training in the Black Belt Basics. I just didn't know it yet.

After I lost my career as a police officer due to a medical retirement, I was devastated. The badge, the brotherhood, the mission—I had to let it all go. What followed wasn't just a career shift. It was a complete identity crisis. I didn't know who I was anymore.

But even in that loss, a new foundation was being laid. Sobriety through AA taught me to take responsibility, to show up with integrity, and to treat every role—no matter how small—with pride, care, and purpose.

That's professionalism. And it became one of the first belts I earned in my new life.

In early recovery, I worked a string of jobs to support my family:

- Security guard
- Paint stocker
- Shoe store clerk
- Magician
- Private investigator

None of these jobs came with prestige. But I didn't treat them as "beneath me." I wore a tie. I stood tall. I arrived early. I did the work 100%. I kept my car clean inside and out—because I believed how I showed up mattered.

Those jobs weren't just ways to make a paycheck.
They were my "dojo".

They taught me discipline, presence, and respect.

These jobs weren't glamorous. They weren't on anyone's highlight reel. But they mattered. They taught me that true professionalism isn't tied to a paycheck or a position. It's how we live. It's how we treat people. Whether you're behind a register, leading a team, cleaning a garage, or helping a struggling child—how you show up is the training, and the integrity.

When I became an insurance agent, I brought that same warrior mindset. I didn't coast. I didn't cut corners. I treated every phone call and every client like it was a test of character.

Within three years, I made the Million Dollar Round Table—not because I was slick, but because I was consistent.

Eventually, I partnered with my father-in-law, Leo, and together we built a thriving agency—one rooted in integrity, honesty, values, and service. He became one of my most trusted mentors. We dressed sharply, spoke respectfully, and treated every client like they were family.

We were always professional, not just for business, but for legacy.

We weren't just building an agency.
We were building trust.

Looking back, that agency was another kind of "dojo". And he was my Sensei—teaching me how to carry myself with humility and class, how to lead with a service mindset, and how to stay steady under pressure.

The belt may have been invisible, but the Black Belt Basics were the same:

- Show up early
- Speak the truth
- Finish what you start
- Treat your name like your uniform

That mindset eventually found its fullest expression when I brought to life our American Martial Arts Academy. From day one, professionalism and integrity were the cornerstones. Not just how we trained—but how we talked, how we listened, how we followed through.

Students often think the Black Belt is the goal. But I know differently.

The Black Belt is just the visible reward for hundreds of unseen moments of professionalism. Integrity. Quiet consistency. Showing up tired. Folding the gi. Repeating the basics. Repeatedly.

That's what makes a person Unshakeable.

Professionalism and integrity form the belt we wear beneath the belt.
They hold everything together.

Crisis or Clarity

I once responded to a tense call as a police officer. A man was holding a pistol in a crowded parking lot, completely out of control. My adrenaline surged. My instinct screamed. But my training held me still. I slowed my breath, scanned the terrain, made eye contact with my partner, and waited for the right moment.
No bullets were fired. No one was hurt. Because we didn't react. We responded!

I approached slowly, my tone calm. I spoke directly but respectfully. I gave him his options, and I let him know that if he needed to talk, I would listen. His shoulders dropped. He took a breath. And then... he lowered the pistol.

We stood there for a long while. Just two men. One broken. One steady.

And we talked.

That wasn't just law enforcement training. That was professionalism in action—under pressure, with a life on the line.

Just like on the mat, life hits hard. A coworker lashes out. A spouse is distant. A diagnosis arrives. The question is: do we react or do we respond?

A warrior doesn't just train to fight. He trains to remain grounded.

That's not just martial arts. That's marriage, recovery, business, and parenthood.

Think Like a Black Belt

In our dojo, we teach students to guard their thoughts like they guard their stance.

Sloppy thinking leads to sloppy techniques and to sloppy living.

The mind is the first battlefield. If we lose there, we'll lose everywhere else.

That's why we train to:

- Pause before reacting
- Choose our response
- Return to principles, not emotions

A white belt may throw a kick.
A Black Belt understands why, when, and if that kick should even be thrown.

Bamboo and the Storm

There's a story I love about a fierce storm that hit a quiet village. Trees were uprooted. Power lines snapped. But one small grove of bamboo remained standing.

Why?

Because bamboo bends—but doesn't break.

Black Belt Mindset is like bamboo.

It knows when to stand firm... and when to bend with wisdom.

It's not rigid ego. It's resilient spirit.

The Samurai and the Mind

An ancient story tells of a young samurai who asked a master monk,
"Master, how do I conquer my enemies?"

The monk pointed to a candle and blew it out.

Then he said,
"Conquer the wind, and you will conquer your enemies."

The samurai looked confused.

The monk added,
"The wind is your mind. If you can't steady it, you'll fight battles that don't exist."

Shihan's Wisdom

Use kindness. Make a call. Keep your word.

These aren't small acts; they're real training.
Because if we can be trusted in the little things, we can be trusted in anything.
That's how you build an Unshakeable life.

Unshakeable Reminder -

The body follows the mind.
The mind must follow something greater—your values, your Higher Power, your purpose.

Train both, and whether you're on the mat, at the dinner table, or facing a storm, you'll move with peace, presence, and power.

"Your Black Belt starts with how you treat the daily jobs.
Fold the uniform. Clean the car. Respect the role.
Show up like a warrior—even if it's just to stock paint."
- Brad Wenneberg, Shihan

Chapter 3 - No Shortcuts to Greatness

"There is no elevator to success — you have to take the stairs."
- Zig Ziglar

Every journey worth making comes with a cost. Becoming a Black Belt—whether on the mat, in life, or in leadership—requires something more than talent or luck. It takes resolve. It takes discipline. It takes a deep decision, made repeatedly, to keep showing up.

I remember a student named Robert. He came to class eager, full of energy—and full of expectations. After two weeks, he asked me, "When do we learn the flying kick?"
I smiled and handed him a broom.
"Right after you master sweeping the mat."

He looked confused.
But he swept.
And he stayed.
One year later, he was leading warm-ups for new students—and teaching them how to sweep the mat with pride.

When people walk into our dojo for the first time, they often ask, "How long does it take to get a black belt?" The real answer is **as long as it takes.**
Because what you're really earning isn't a belt—it's a mindset.
A way of life.

What it takes is the willingness to fail, and to fail often.
To mess up in front of others.

To fall and get up with dignity.
To stay when it's boring.
To persevere when no one is watching.

What it takes is **grit**.

In my recovery journey, I found that the same traits apply. Sobriety doesn't happen in a single decision—it happens daily, in the quiet moments when no one else would know if you slipped. It takes what I call **"stubborn humility"**—the unshakeable belief that you can grow, paired with the humility to admit when you need help.

That kind of humility doesn't always show up politely.
Sometimes it arrives in tears.
Sometimes in a sponsor's number on speed dial.
Sometimes it looks like a whisper, "I can't do this alone," even after years of doing it your way.
But that combination—grit and grace—is what keeps us sober, strong, and sane.
In business, I've learned that what it takes to grow a team, or a dream, is
Trust. **Integrity**. **Accountability**.
You can't fake it long-term.
People follow consistency more than charisma.

As a parent and a grandparent, what it takes is **Love**. **Presence**.
Listening when you're tired.
Showing up when you're busy.
Giving grace when you want to give corrections.

In martial arts, students come in wanting fast results.
They want power without process.

But the truth is, nothing great comes easy.
And nothing worthwhile is handed out.

What it takes is what no one else sees.
The hours on the mat after class is over.
The repetition of the same technique until it becomes second nature.
The choice to keep going when it would be easier to quit.

No Shortcuts

Let me tell you about one of the most meaningful "no shortcuts" stories of my career.

It was a hot summer night when two related families walked into my dojo—seven people total, including two adults and five children. I was just beginning to build my student body, and truthfully, I was still trying to breathe financially. My first month's profit had been a whopping sixteen dollars. So, to say I was excited about this group joining would be an understatement.

But there was a challenge: they had just emigrated from Russia. They didn't speak English very well. They were new to our culture, new to the country, and unfamiliar with martial arts. Through an interpreter, they explained they hoped to learn karate—not just to protect themselves, but also to learn English.

Yikes, I thought. *I teach karate—not language arts.*

I told them I'd give it some thought and call them that evening. I sat in my office running numbers, thinking how this one enrollment could help relieve the pressure I was under. But then clear as a lightning bolt, it hit me.

"You didn't open this dojo to make money. You opened it to serve. The money is a byproduct of five-star classes and service."

So, I took off the banker's hat and put on the service hat.

I called my mentor, hoping for some guidance. He admitted he had never faced anything quite like this—but gave me the best advice: "Do your research. Then follow your heart."

I sat in that office for hours, creating a plan. I decided I would teach them—karate, culture, and language—if they were willing to trust me. That night, I called them back. They said yes. And the very next day, they bowed in.

I developed a system using three tools: my **words**, my **gestures**, and **positive reinforcement**. I didn't water anything down. They still had to learn the Japanese phrases we use in class, just like every other student. But I caught them succeeding ten times more often than I corrected them. I made it fun. I made it consistent. And I made sure they knew they belonged.

Slowly, they began to form better sentences. They picked up stronger English—and yes, a little Japanese too. We helped them with school projects, filled out job applications with them, and even guided them on how to navigate daily life in a new country.

They never quit. That's what struck me most. They faced every obstacle with determination, joy, and trust. In the end, *five of the seven earned their Black Belts*. The two adults, Alex and David, became incredible instructors and key team members. They stayed with our studio for decades. They helped build the very foundation of what we are today.

A Fun Story - Shihan & Alex in "The Sting"
(Yes, this really happened.)

Back in the early days of the studio, I was still learning the ropes as a business owner. One afternoon, I met with a representative from a well-known, prestigious newspaper to place an ad. We discussed placement, pricing, and after some friendly negotiation, agreed on a solid deal.

As he stood to leave, the rep casually mentioned that if I paid in cash, I'd get an extra 10% off that month's price.

Cash? From a national paper?

Something didn't sit right. But hey, I was new to business—and saving money sounded good. I figured I'd sleep on it.

Later that evening, during adult class, it hit me like a spinning back kick to the gut: *Why would a major publication ask for cash?* That's when I called over my good friend Alex—who, at the time, had recently moved to the U.S. from Russia and was still adjusting to American life (and language), and learning the martial arts.

I laid it out for him. He nodded thoughtfully and said, "Call them tomorrow. Let's see what's up."

The next morning, I made the call.

Turns out, this guy wasn't with the paper anymore. Worse, he was under suspicion for a string of armed robberies and was going around collecting "cash payments" from small businesses before skipping town.

So, I did what any sober, karate-practicing former police officer might do—I suggested a 'sting'.

I contacted the local detectives and offered to wire up the dojo. We placed hidden cameras around the studio and even had two undercover officers dressed in karate uniforms, just in case.

Alex, bless his heart, was still confused about what was happening but was totally on board. He played his part perfectly. When the suspect arrived, Alex greeted him warmly, made small talk, and led him into my office, where I waited.

We kept it casual. A few golf jokes, some fake paperwork, then I went through my rehearsed lines. I said, "So just to be clear—you're giving me 10% off for paying in cash, right?"
He nodded. "Yes, sir."

The moment the cash exchanged hands, the detectives burst in. The guy resisted, but they took him down fast.

Later, after things calmed down, Alex looked at me, eyes wide with excitement, and said in his thick Russian accent:

"That was *bitchen.* Can we do it again someday?"

Classic.

The sting worked. The suspect was convicted for robbery and theft-related charges; but what stuck with me most was Alex's joy in the chaos. For a man new to this country, his heart, his loyalty, and his willingness to serve were nothing short of heroic.

And that's part of what this chapter is really about - **showing up, doing the work, and standing tall even when things get messy.**
There are no shortcuts. But there are great stories.
Especially if you have a Russian sidekick who thinks stings are "*bitchen*."
Alex became one of my dearest friends.
We trained hard.
We laughed harder.
And then, one day, we cried.

Alex passed away several years ago from a brain tumor. It devastated us.

When his family was deciding what to put on his headstone, they asked if I had a suggestion.

This is what we etched in stone:

"Alex – Second-Degree Black Belt and
One of the Founding Members of Goju Shin-Ryu."

That's greatness.
No shortcuts.
Just heart, perseverance, and the courage to keep showing up.

Unshakeable Reminder -

The journey asks everything of us—not all at once, but day by day.

Are we willing to give our best even when the rewards aren't immediate?
What it takes is often less about ability—and more about **staying power**.

Chapter 4 - Strong Stance, Steady Spirit

"It is not the strength of the body that counts, but the strength of the spirit."
- J.R.R. Tolkien

Every Black Belt begins as a white belt—unsure, awkward, and often overwhelmed.
I've been there.
But here's the secret I've discovered.
White belts who master the basics become Black Belts who master life.

In our dojo, the basics aren't just warm-ups or drills. They're sacred.

They are the stance.
The breath.
The bow.
The focus.
Without them, everything else crumbles.
A flashy kick without proper balance?
Just a fall waiting to happen.

When I first stepped into a dojo, I thought I had to prove myself. But over time, I realized it wasn't about *proving*—it was about *improving*.

And improvement only happened when I humbled myself enough to start with the basics... and stay with them.

In recovery, my basics were honesty, humility, and accountability.

In business, it meant showing up early, doing what I said I would do, and cleaning the toilets when no one else would.

As a husband, father, and friend, it meant listening more than I talked, keeping my word, and putting people before my preferences.

The Foundation Test

Many years ago, we were hosting a Black Belt test. Several students were going for their first-degree Black Belt. Others, already Black Belts, were testing for a higher rank.

One of those candidates had traveled from our associated school in San Jose. Before the test began, I noticed him in the far corner of the dojo. He wasn't warming up with flashy kicks or fancy moves. He was working on fundamentals—**white belt material**. Front stances. Simple blocks. Slow, precise, focused.

Then he knelt facing the corner, closed his eyes, and meditated silently for five minutes.

When the test started, this student stood tall, calm, and ready. He didn't appear nervous, he looked *centered*. Prepared.

The test was long. Four grueling hours. No breaks. No shortcuts. As others began to fade, this student remained sharp, crisp in every move. Consistent. Grounded. Precise. Disciplined.

Toward the end, even he began to show signs of exhaustion. The toll was visible. But he didn't give in. He had trained for this. Not just the advanced techniques—he had trained the **basics**.

Because the basics demand **daily discipline,** they're not necessarily glamorous—but they pay dividends.

When we finished and began announcing promotions, this student suddenly bolted off the mat and ran into the bathroom. Moments later, we found him... throwing up into the toilet.

Without hesitation, every Black Belt on our team followed me in. And right there—while he was hugging porcelain—I awarded him his new rank.

That's what excellence looks like.
That's what happens when the basics become a part of us.
He did the work. He respected the process. He became unshakeable.

"The roots of a strong spirit grow in the soil of daily discipline."
— Brad Wenneberg, Shihan

A strong stance brings balance. But a **steady spirit** brings *center*.

That inner calm? That's where real strength lives.
It's the quiet resolve we draw from adversity.
The calm breath when chaos surrounds us.
The humility begins again.
The fire finishes strong.

We bow before we begin—not just to show respect, but to **center ourselves**.

When life tests us, flashy skills don't carry the day.
But presence does.

Peace does.
A steady spirit does.

That student didn't just have talent—he had **spiritual discipline**. He entered the test grounded. He left it physically empty because he gave it his all, but full of honor.

To me, that's what makes a martial artist, a leader, a warrior—not just the stance of the body, but the **stance of the soul**.

Over the years, I've taught thousands of students. The ones who truly succeed aren't always the most gifted, they're the most consistent.

They honor the basics.
They take their time.
They build their foundation silently, patiently, powerfully.

A child learning how to bow properly is learning **respect**.
A beginner struggling through a front stance is building **discipline**.

These simple actions, repeated with care, build a base no storm can destroy.

I've seen it - Black Belts who drift from the basics become hollow. But white belts who cling to them?

They become *unshakeable*.

Excellence—real, lasting excellence—is built on simple things:
Honesty.
Consistency.
Humility.
Effort.

These are the *Black Belt Basics*.
When we practice them with intention, we're ready for life's biggest tests—on and off the mat.

In my experience, how we begin often shapes how far we'll go.

So, in our personal growth, our relationships, our work, our recovery, and our faith—I believe in honoring the basics.

This is how we build a Black Belt life—
One strong, steady step at a time,
strengthening our spirit as we go.

"You don't rise to the level of your goals.
You fall to the level of your systems."
— James Clear

Unshakeable Reminder -

The basics are bowing. The spirit is the breath.
One grounds us. The other guides us.

Today I ask myself -
Am I rooted in daily fundamentals—and rising from spiritual center?

True mastery lives in the student who trains the stance *and* the soul.

"Spiritual progress doesn't mean we never fall—it means we rise a little stronger each time."
- Brad Wenneberg, Shihan

Chapter 5 - Character Over Credentials

"Ability may get us to the top,
but it takes character to keep us there."
- John Wooden

I've known martial artists with wall-to-wall trophies who couldn't lead a class with humility.
I've met Black Belts with perfect form and no patience.
And I've met white belts who showed up with a quiet character that humbled the entire room.

Skills matter. Credentials open doors.
But character? That's what keeps them open.

In the dojo and in life, I've learned that what truly counts is:

Who we are when no one is watching.
What we do when it's hard.
How we treat people who can do nothing for us.
How we carry ourselves when we win... and how we rise when we lose.

One of my biggest breakthroughs came when I stopped trying to be impressive—and started trying to be useful.
I didn't want to just *have* a black belt.
I wanted to *live like* a Black Belt.

That meant showing up early, owning my mistakes, apologizing when needed.

It meant helping someone else shine instead of hogging the spotlight.

"My uniform doesn't make me a leader. My attitude does."

People don't always remember the kata or the kicks.
But they remember how we made them feel.
They remember whether our handshake matched our word—and whether our belt matched our behavior.

Whether on the mat, in recovery, in family life, or in business—credentials might start the conversation, but it's our character that finishes it well.

I've learned to train my mind, train my body.
But more than anything, I've had to train my heart.

The Real Rank Test

Over time, I've come to believe that character is the *real* test. Not just once a year at a belt exam—but every day.

Here are some of the lessons I've had to practice repeatedly:

- I follow through on what I say I'll do—even when it's inconvenient.
- I remind myself to treat people with respect, no matter what their rank or role.
- I strive to speak the truth, but with love—not ego.
- I own my mistakes fast and don't waste time defending them.

- I aim to lift others as I climb—because that's what real Black Belts do.

"We can polish the belt all we want—but if the heart's tarnished, it won't shine."
- Lesson from the dojo floor

Character in Action: The Wheelchair Warrior

Back in 1992, shortly after opening my dojo, a 21-year-old man rolled into my office in a wheelchair.

He had recently been in a terrible car accident. He'd been drinking at a party, got into an argument with his girlfriend, and drove off in a rage—foot to the floor, emotions in the driver's seat. Less than a block away, he lost control and hit a tree. The crash left him paralyzed from the chest down.

He could still use his arms, but his entire life had been turned upside down. He told me, "I need help learning how to live again. I've been to other dojos, but they turned me away. They didn't know what to do with me."

I looked at him and said, "I don't know how to help either... but together, we'll figure it out."

And we did.

He trained and taught for four years. He earned his advanced brown belt.
He got married. He had two beautiful children.
Though he passed away in his forties, he lived like a warrior—

defined not by what he'd lost, but by the spirit he refused to let go of.

At his celebration of life, I had the honor of presenting his black belt to his father. It wasn't just a symbol of what he had done on the mat—it was a symbol of what he had overcome.

Lighthearted Confession from the Journey

One day in his early training with me, his wife pulled me aside and said, "He always asks me to help him up the stairs at night. But I know he can do it himself."

I smiled and gave her an idea. "Tonight, stand at the top of the stairs... completely naked. When he asks for help, just say, 'Come and get it.'"

The next day she came in grinning from ear to ear.
"He zipped up those stairs faster than ever."

Now *that* is motivation. And *that* is character.

> *"Talent might get you in the door,*
> *but it's your character that keeps you in the room."*
> - Morris Chestnut

What My Black Belt Doesn't Say

My black belt doesn't tell the whole story.

It doesn't say how many times I almost quit.
It doesn't say how many failures I had to rise from—or how many mornings I tied that belt around a body that felt broken and a spirit that felt small.

Unshakeable

It doesn't say how long I spent as a white belt, doubting if I belonged here at all.
It doesn't reveal the nights I lay awake wondering if I was good enough, strong enough, or worthy of the title.
It doesn't mention the mistakes I made as a leader, or how many apologies it took to become one that people trusted.

It doesn't show the tears I've hidden in the locker room, the heartbreaks I brought to the mat, or the quiet prayers I said before bowing in.
It doesn't show the people who mentored me... or the ones I let down before I knew better.
It doesn't tell the story of redemption.

What it *does* say—without words—is that I kept going.
That I chose to stand back up, repeatedly.
That I traded ego for growth, applause for accountability, and shortcuts for the long, slow road of transformation.

So, when I tie my black belt around my waist today, I don't wear it as a badge of perfection.
I wear it as a reminder:

Of whom I was.
Of who I am still becoming.
And of the kind of warrior I want to be when no one's watching.

"My belt may be black—but the lessons that built it came in every color."
- Brad Wenneberg, Shihan

Unshakeable Reminder -

Titles fade. Belts fray.
But character? Character endures.

Let's keep asking ourselves:

- Am I living in alignment with what I believe?
- Am I honoring my words, even when it's hard?
- Am I treating people the way I hope to be remembered?

True rank isn't worn. It's lived.
Let our belts be symbols—not just of what we've achieved—but of who we've become.

"Be the kind of person our belt would be proud to be tied around."
- Brad Wenneberg, Shihan

Chapter 6 - Offense Is a Choice

"You can't control the first thought.
But you can control the second."
- Recovery Wisdom

Some people walk through life waiting to be offended.
They scan every word, every look, every delay, every offhand comment for proof that someone has disrespected them. And when they find it—because they always find it—they react. Hard.

Here's the truth I've learned the hard way:
Offense is not automatic. It's optional.

Just because someone serves it, doesn't mean you have to swing.

In martial arts, we train to be ready for attack.
But we also train for **control**—of our breathing, our emotions, and our decisions.

We teach students that real power isn't about domination.
It's about discernment.

Just because you can throw a punch doesn't mean you should.
Just because you can retaliate doesn't mean that's strength.

Sometimes the strongest move is **no move at all**.

The Mental Tennis Match

Sometimes life feels like a tennis match—
Back and forth, insult for insult, sarcasm for sarcasm, judgment for judgment.

They serve it...
And we swing back.

But what if we just **caught the ball**?

What if we simply held it in our hand, looked at the person across the net, and said,
"I'm done playing this game."

Offense is a choice.
Participation is a choice.
And walking away? That's not weakness—it's **wisdom**.

Not every match needs a winner.
Some battles are best won by refusing to battle at all.

In the dojo, we don't just teach how to fight—
We teach **when not to**.

We train to respond, not react.

Let's practice that off the mat too.
Let's learn to recognize the volley...
And instead of swinging back, let's **catch the ball and walk away**.

That's not giving up.
That's leveling up.

I've learned this lesson the hard way, especially in recovery.

I used to get offended by everything.
The guy who cut me off, the person who talked too much, the friend who didn't say thank you.
I could turn almost anything into a justification for resentment.

In sobriety, I've learned that **resentment is the poison I drink hoping someone else will die**.
It doesn't hurt them, it hurts me.
It pollutes my peace.
And it invites me back into the emotional tennis match I've worked so hard to walk away from.

In marriage, I've learned this too.

Bonnie and I don't agree on everything.
Shocker, right?

But I've learned that I don't have to return every serve.
Not every eye roll needs a speech.
Not every silence needs to be filled.

Sometimes the greatest gift I can give to my marriage is **not swinging back**.

Same with business.
Same with parenting.
Same with life.

Ancient Wisdom: The Silent Samurai

There's an old tale of a samurai who was insulted by a drunk in the street.

The drunk stumbled toward him, slurred an insult, and mocked the warrior's sword and honor.

The samurai had every right—and every skill—to cut him down where he stood.

But he didn't.

He simply bowed, stepped aside, and continued on his way.

Later, when asked why he didn't retaliate, he replied:

"Why should I let someone else decide when I draw my sword?"

The real warrior knows that responding to insult with violence is not mastery—
it's slavery to ego.

The world will always hand us insults and offenses.
But no one can make us carry them.

"In the moment of action,
the difference between impulse and intention
defines the warrior."
- Unknown Samurai Proverb

Unshakeable Reminder -

They may 'serve it', but you don't have to swing.
Catch the ball. Walk away. Train your peace like you train your punches.
Offense is a choice—and wisdom is the better weapon.

"You don't earn rank by taking offense.
You earn it by letting go of what doesn't serve your peace."
- Brad Wenneberg, Shihan

Chapter 7 - Defense Wins Championships

"The ultimate aim of martial arts is not having to use them."
- Miyamoto Musashi

Defense is just as important as offense—sometimes more.
It's not a weakness. It's wisdom.
It's the strength to protect what matters.

Street Safety Starts with Smart Choices

The best self-defense? Avoiding the fight altogether.

As martial artists, we train for the worst but live for the best. That means staying aware of our surroundings, trusting our instincts, and not putting ourselves in risky situations.

Defense begins long before a punch is thrown.
It begins with wise decisions.

Walk with purpose.
Don't go where trouble lives.
True Black Belts don't need to prove anything—they plan ahead and walk away with honor.

In the dojo, defense is about awareness, timing, and control.
A well-timed block can neutralize the strongest punch.

In life, it means setting boundaries, guarding our time, and choosing our influences wisely.

Street Control: A Cop's Guide to Defense

During my years as a patrolman, I'm proud to say this:
I never had to engage in a physical fight with a suspect.

Yes, I restrained many individuals—but never out of ego or escalation.
There were plenty of times I *could have* upped the ante... but I chose not to.

While some officers seemed eager to make an example out of someone, I took a different approach.

At 5'6", I was often the smallest person on the scene.
But what I lacked in size, I made up for in **command presence**.

My posture, my tone, my calm confidence made one thing very clear:
If this goes past a certain point, I *will* act—and I *will* act decisively.

But first, I gave them a way out.

I used a tone that was **commanding, not demanding**.
I let the suspect save face, even as they were being handcuffed.
My body language stayed relaxed and in control.

I didn't threaten—I set boundaries. I offered dignity, but I made it clear:
Comply now, or the next step will be very painful.

Most people chose to comply.

Other officers didn't always understand.
"Why talk someone down when you have every right to take them down?"

Because talking them down was smarter. Safer. More professional. Fighting when I could have de-escalated? That wasn't strength, that was stupidity.

I'm proud of that record.
No brawls. No bruises. No broken bones.
Just steady tone, thoughtful choices, and clean arrests.
That same restraint has served me well beyond the badge.

Because defense isn't about hiding—it's about holding the line with wisdom.

Calm Beats Flashy

I've seen it on the mat:
The students who stay calm under pressure, protect their centerline, and stay grounded—those are the ones who outlast the flash.

Defense isn't flashy.
But it's the glue that holds the fight together.

Offense might win points.
But defense wins championships.

Defense means learning to say no—to distractions, temptations, and detours from our path.
It means knowing our values... and standing by them, even when it's inconvenient.

Sometimes the most powerful thing we can do is walk away.
Not out of fear—but out of strength.

Timeless Tactics: Ancient Lessons in Defense

Horatius at the Bridge – Rome, 6th Century BC

In the early days of the Roman Republic, Publius Horatius Cocles stood at the narrow entrance of the Pons Sublician Bridge. A massive Etruscan army approached the gates of Rome.

Rather than attack, Horatius and two comrades held the bridge long enough for Roman soldiers to destroy it behind them. As the bridge neared destruction, Horatius sent his companions back to safety while he remained alone to face the entire Etruscan army.

Once the bridge was demolished, Horatius, still fully armed, leaped into the Tiber River and swam to the other side. He was able to swim to safety, fulfilling his mission and saving Rome.

He didn't win by fighting - he won by *defending*, holding the line when it mattered most.

Lesson for us: We don't need to charge into every conflict. Sometimes, standing firm—and knowing when to retreat—can save everything.

The Lute-Playing General – Ancient China

A famous Chinese general once found himself defending a town with only 100 men against an approaching army of 150,000.

Instead of barricading the gates or preparing for battle, he opened the gates wide, seated himself on the wall, and calmly played a lute.

The opposing general, fearing a trap, turned his entire army around and left.

No violence. No bloodshed.
Just a show of calm, confident control.

Lesson for us: We don't always need muscle to win the moment. Sometimes, calmness and confidence disarm chaos faster than any technique.

What I'm Still Defending Today

- I still defend my mornings—from negativity and noise.
- I still defend my sobriety—from whispers and memories.
- I still defend my peace—from chaos, conflict, and comparison.
- I still defend the dojo—from ego, shortcuts, and excuses.
- I still defend my family—from neglect and distraction.
- And I defend my mission—from anything that tries to blur my purpose.

The threats change.
The defense must evolve.
But the calling stays the same: **protect what matters.**

Unshakeable Reminder –

Ancient warriors teach us:

- Holding the line with discipline can save a city.

- Calm resolve can turn away armies without a strike.

And we recognize the same truth today:

Defense isn't weakness—it's wisdom.

We stay alert. We set boundaries. We guard our peace.
We choose our battles—and refuse those that don't belong to us.

Sometimes the strongest move is the one we never make.

- Am I protecting what truly matters?
- Am I saying yes too often—and no too little?
- Am I chasing battles that don't belong to me?

We must guard our peace, defend our growth, and protect our energy.
Because sometimes, **survival is the victory.**
And sometimes, **the greatest strength is not striking—but standing still.**

"The wise warrior avoids the battle
others waste their lives chasing."
- Sun Tzu, ancient Chinese general

Chapter 8 - Focus Is the Superpower of a Warrior

*"The successful warrior is the average man,
with laser-like focus."*
- Bruce Lee

In a world full of noise, distraction, and constant comparison, it's easy to lose sight of what matters. Focus is what brings clarity in chaos. It's the quiet force that allows us to tune out the static, and zero in on what really counts.

When I step onto the mat, everything else fades away.
The bills.
The headlines.
The noise.

All gone.

What's left is *now*. The breath. The stance. The technique.
The stillness before the strike.

A Mind Like Water

In martial arts, we train to be fully present.
To be in a clear, calm, and focused mental state.

Still water can ripple when disturbed but always returns to its natural state of calm.

We block what doesn't serve us, and channel our energy into what does.
That's focus—not just intensity, but **intention**.

When I was rebuilding my life—through sobriety, business, and personal transformation—I couldn't afford to be scattered.

I had to learn to say "**no**" to what looked good in order to say "**yes**" to what was best.

That meant no to shortcuts.
No to people who drained my spirit.
No to habits that numbed rather than healed.

It meant yes to structure.
Yes to growth.
Yes to living on purpose.

Focus Doesn't Eliminate Temptation—It Repositions It

Let me be clear - focus doesn't make life easier.
But it does make **life clearer**.

When I wake up each morning, I still must choose where I place my attention.
Will I focus on gratitude... or grumble about what's not perfect?
Will I stay committed to my values... or drift toward distraction?

I've learned this the hard way:
What I feed, grows. What I starve, dies.

So, I try to feed my purpose.
Starve the distractions.
And focus on progress, not perfection.

The Bamboo Lesson

There's a story of a martial arts master who took a student deep into the bamboo forest. He asked the student, "What do you see?"

The student looked around and replied, "A thousand things—trees, insects, sunlight, birds."

The master said nothing.

Later, he brought the student to the same spot, this time blindfolded him, and had him breathe for ten minutes. Then he asked again, "What do you see?"

The student said, "I see... just the bamboo."

The master nodded. "Good. That's the difference between looking—and focusing."

Focus narrows the field.
It silences the unnecessary.
It reveals what matters most.

My Student Taught Me This

I once asked a student preparing for his Black Belt test, "What's your biggest strength?"
Without hesitation, he said, "Focus. I may not be the fastest or strongest, but I don't get distracted."

And he was right.

He didn't bounce around.
He didn't chase applause.
He chased progress.

He passed his test with power and grace—not because of his speed, but because of his **mindset**.

The Noisy World

We live in a world that profits from distraction.
The scroll. The ping. The pressure to do more, be more, want more.

But warriors train differently.

We train to lock in.
To say no with power.
To stay centered when the storm swirls around us.

I remind myself often:
Don't chase ten rabbits. Track one.

The day gets clearer when the mission gets smaller.

Unshakeable Reminder –

Focus isn't just about what we look at—
It's about what we choose to ignore.

Distractions will always chase us,
but clarity allows us to stand still in the storm.

Let's ask ourselves:

- Are we locked in on what truly matters?

- Or letting noise pull us off course?
- Are we focused on work or worry?

Let's sharpen our sight.
Let's anchor our actions.
Let's strike with intention—not impulse.

In the dojo, as in business, in recovery, and in life—
focus wins.

"Clarity is the antidote to anxiety."
- Marcus Buckingham

Chapter 9 - Right Size

"Some of us can be face down in the gutter and still look down on the rest of the world."
- AA Wisdom

I remember the first time I read the phrase "right size" in AA literature.
I had to stop and reread it.
Right size? What does *that* even mean?

At the time, I was all over the map.
I had two settings: inflated or deflated.

I was either the biggest ego in the room or the most miserable one.
A taker. A user. A master manipulator.

Even when I was completely broken, I could still find a way to think that I was better than someone else.

They say some of us can be face down in the gutter and still look down on the rest of the world.
That was me.

The Two Ends of the Same Stick

I've learned over the years that being "too big" or "too small" is really the same character defect with different costumes.
Self-righteousness and self-pity come from the same root: **self-centeredness**.

Sometimes I was arrogant and judgmental — thinking I knew better than everyone else.
Rigid. Unteachable. Punitive.

Other times I was so stuck in self-pity I could barely move.
Depressed. Blaming the world.
Throwing myself a pity party with full catering.

Neither one was *right size*.

Right size isn't about thinking less of yourself — it's about being honest about who and what you are.
It's spiritual. It's emotional. It's practical.

I didn't come to understand that overnight.
It took years of trial and error — and some serious humbling.

The Dojo, the Ego, and the Downfall

When I opened my first martial arts studio, I had a mentor I deeply respected.
He gave me one piece of advice I'll never forget:

"Brad — don't hang any pictures of yourself in the dojo. This isn't about you. It's about service."

I followed that advice. For a while.

But over time, my head started to swell.
The studio was growing. Students respected me. People admired what I was building.
And that old gorilla — the one named **Ego** — came back swinging.

I started putting myself at the center.
I made it about me.

And when that happened, the foundation cracked.
I relapsed.
Drank.
Everything started to unravel — personally, professionally, spiritually.

It was a disaster.
But it was also a wake-up call.

Climbing Out of the "Poor Me's"

So how do we climb out when we've sunk too low?
How do we get unstuck when we've slid into self-pity?

Here's what I've learned:

1. Service is the Exit Door

When I'm in self-pity, my world shrinks.
But when I do something for someone else — hold a door, say a kind word, mop the mats, call someone who's hurting — I reconnect with something bigger than me.
That's spiritual alignment. That's right size.

2. Move a Muscle, Change a Mood

Even when I don't *feel* like doing anything... I do something anyway.
Clean. Walk. Bow in.
Motion triggers momentum.

3. Call Someone and Don't Talk About Yourself

The ego loves attention — even *negative* attention.
When I reach out to someone with zero agenda and ask, "How are *you* doing?" — the pity party ends.

4. Gratitude is the Sword That Slays Self-Pity

I can't be truly grateful and miserable at the same time.
When I feel the "poor me's" creeping in, I list five things I'm grateful for.
Out loud. On paper. Doesn't matter how small.
"I'm sober."
"I get another shot."
"My grandkids laugh when they see me."

That's enough to shift me. Every time.

Honest Work, Humble Heart

Getting back to "right size" didn't come from punishment — it came from *honest work*.
I had to face myself.
I had to admit my character defects.
I had to ask for help.

I had to stop faking it and start *living it*.
Be vulnerable. Teachable. Willing.

Not just talk about humility — *practice* it.
Not just preach service — *live* it.
Not just say "palms up" — actually show up with my palms up.

And day by day, I learned:
It's not about me.
Not then. Not now. Not ever.

Right size isn't a one-time fix.
It's a daily decision.
It's how I show up at home, in the dojo, and in my spirit.

Watch That Gorilla

That ego of mine? He didn't die.
He's in the corner doing pushups, just waiting for me to let my guard down.

If I rest on my laurels…
If I start thinking I've got it all figured out…
If I forget to ask for help or stop showing up in service…
He'll come back.

And he's not just annoying — he's lethal.

He'll cost me my sobriety.
My marriage.
My family.
My students.
My business.
My reputation.
My life.

That's how serious this is.

So, every morning, I ask for help.
Every day, I reset.

And every time I bow in, I remind myself why I started:
To serve.
To love.
To live right sized.

"Ego is just an overdressed fear."
- Brandi Carlile

Unshakeable Reminder -

Right size means knowing the truth about yourself — not inflated, not deflated, just honest.
It means taking responsibility for your growth, your choices, and your service to others.
Stay humble. Stay teachable.

Stay right-sized — one day, one bow, one breath at a time.

Chapter 10 - The Warrior's Clock

"The key is not in spending time, but in investing it."
- Stephen R. Covey

"One of his students asked Buddha, 'Are you the messiah?'
'No,' answered Buddha.
'Then are you a healer?'
'No,' Buddha replied.
'Then are you a teacher?' the student persisted.
'No, I am not a teacher.'
'Then what are you?' asked the student, exasperated.
'I am awake,' Buddha replied."

Time is one of the most valuable gifts we have - and how we spend it reveals what we truly value.

In martial arts, every belt, every form, every sparring round is earned with time. Not just calendar time, but committed, focused, and purposeful time.

T.I.M.E. is an acronym I use with students and leaders alike:

T – Training: You must be willing to practice. To sweat. To fall and get up again. In life, just like in martial arts, there's no substitute for time on the mat.

I – Integrity: How do we use our time when no one is watching? That's where true growth happens. Show up early. Stay late. Keep promises—to others and to ourselves.

M – Mindset: What we think about most is where our time will go. Guard thoughts, direct focus, and cultivate a mindset that fuels rather than drains.

E – Energy: Time without energy is wasted. Sleep well. Eat right. Move your body. Meditate. Serve. These are investments—not expenses. They fuel our ability to make time count.

I've wasted time before. I've let hours slip by in worry, regret, or avoidance. But I've also learned that the time I spend in prayer, in training, in service, and in stillness—that time always pays off.

We don't need more hours in the day. We need to use the hours we have with more intention.

The next time we feel like we don't have time—remember this: our lives are made of time. How we use it is how we build our legacy.

Make T.I.M.E. count.

"Wherever you are, be there."
- Jim Elliot

One day after an AA meeting, a friend commented on how time goes by so fast. He said, "Vacations are cool, but before you know it—your home." Another added, "My kids are growing up so fast I can't keep up."
I've made those same comments.

But that night I sat with it... and realized that time wasn't moving too fast—it was that I wasn't noticing time.

Unshakeable

I remembered sitting in class as a boy, staring at the clock on the wall thinking, "Only five more minutes till the bell rings."

Time seemed to crawl. But now? It's flying. Why?

Because back then - I was present.

"Lost time is never found again."
- Benjamin Franklin

Now, I'm often preoccupied—reliving yesterday or forecasting tomorrow - and in doing so, I miss *now.*

That little realization shifted something big in me. I decided to slow down—not physically, but mentally and spiritually. To be awake. To *notice.*

Time hasn't changed. I have.

So, I made a commitment: I would enjoy the second. The moment. The breath. I wouldn't miss what's unfolding right in front of me.

Time is consistent. It's me—and how I use the 86,400 seconds of each day—that makes the difference... if I truly take time to be 'awake'.

"You will never always be motivated,
so you must learn to be disciplined."
- Tim Grover

Unshakeable Reminder -

Time is not just what we spend—it's what we shape. Let's ask ourselves: Are we investing in what truly matters, or just staying busy?

"Today is a blank canvas. Let's use it to create something meaningful, moment by moment."
- Brad Wenneberg, Shihan

"Time is what we want most, but what we use worst."
- William Penn

"Your future is created by what you do today—not tomorrow."
- Robert Kiyosaki

"When the student stops watching the clock and starts watching the moment... that's when the real training begins."
- philosophy of Bruce Lee

Chapter 11 - Burning the Grudges, Building the Bridges

"Resentment burns the soul. Amends build the spirit."
- Recovery Wisdom

Clearing the Wreckage

The moment I got sober, I knew I had to do more than stop drinking. I had to clean house—internally and externally. I had to make things right.

In recovery, we talk about *clearing away the wreckage of our past*. For me, that meant confronting the pain I'd caused others, letting go of resentments that poisoned my heart, and learning how to live in the present instead of dragging the past behind me like a corpse.

*"Look not mournfully into the past, it comes not back again.
Wisely improve the present, it is thine."*
- Henry Wadsworth Longfellow

Living in the past is emotional quicksand. You can't build anything from there. I had to get my feet back under me—to step into the now.

Living Amends, Not Just Saying Sorry

I've yelled at my wife. I've broken promises. I've hurt people I love. And I've learned that "sorry" means very little when the behavior doesn't change.

A real amends isn't an apology—it's a lifestyle change.
When I committed to recovery, I made a silent vow: **My dojo would be part of my amends.**

During my drinking days, I lied, I stole, I skipped out on responsibilities. When I got sober, I knew I needed to build something that gave more than it took - something that would serve others and restore what I'd broken.

Every lesson, every belt test is part of that promise.
I don't just run a business, I run a daily act of repentance and restoration.
This place isn't about me. It's about the people we serve.

"Don't tell me your words—show me your walk."
- AA Wisdom

"You cannot do a kindness too soon, for you never know how soon it will be too late."- Ralph Waldo Emerson

"I slept and dreamed that life was joy.
I awoke and saw that life was service.
I acted—and behold, service was joy."
- Rabindranath Tagore

The Poison WE Carry

Resentment is re-living the same wound repeatedly. It's like holding a Styrofoam cup. At first, no big deal. But hold it for an hour... two hours... a week... a year—and it becomes unbearably heavy.

I once had a resentment over something I thought a man said to me. I let it stew for decades. I rehearsed the confrontation in my mind. I waited for the day I could finally put him in his place.

Thirty years later, I finally confronted him.

He looked at me, puzzled, and said:
"Brad, I honestly don't remember saying anything like that. I wouldn't have."

It hit me like a punch to the gut.

He hadn't thought about me or that moment in *thirty years*.
But I had. I carried it like a brick in my soul while he lived free.

"Resentment is like setting yourself on fire and hoping the other person dies of smoke inhalation."
- Anne Lamott, and - Al-Anon Wisdom

Amends aren't just about what we've done to others.
They're also about what we've allowed to rot inside us.

Unshakeable Solutions: Releasing Resentment

So how do we let go?

Here are some Black Belt Basics I've learned:

- **Pray for them**, especially when you don't want to.
- **Own your part**, even if it's small.
- **Write it down** and burn it. Release it symbolically.
- **Talk it through with a mentor.**

- **Serve someone else.** You can't resent and serve at the same time.

You can't wrestle resentment with willpower alone.
You fight it with *spiritual firepower.*

Forgiveness isn't approval.
It's *freedom*—yours, not theirs.

Carrying the Message

Living amends is more than behavior—it's presence. It's energy. It's the way I walk through life now.

If I don't share the gifts I've been given, they stagnate. I can't keep what I don't give away. Amends means giving back what grace has given me.

I ask myself regularly:

- What do I have to offer?
- What example am I setting?
- Am I attracting people with purpose?
- Is my life a blessing?

I don't want to just feel better—I want to live better.

"The ultimate measure of a man is not where he stands in moments of comfort, but where he stands at times of challenge and controversy."
- Dr. Martin Luther King Jr.

Each of us has a choice: let our past destroy us—or let it make us stronger.
I choose strength.
I choose healing.
I choose to become a blessing—not a burden.

Even as a kid, I knew the buck had to stop somewhere.
I decided it would stop with me.

Ancient Story: The Two Monks and the Woman

Two monks were walking through the countryside when they came to a river, where a woman stood unable to cross.

Without hesitation, the older monk picked her up and carried her across.

Hours later, the younger monk said, "How could you carry her? We're not supposed to touch women!"

The older monk replied:
"I put her down hours ago. Why are you still carrying her?"

Resentment is often something we were never meant to carry in the first place.

Miracles in Motion

Amends work. They heal. They rebuild. I've seen it firsthand.

At the dojo, I've seen students walk in carrying pain—and walk out carrying purpose.

There was a woman years ago—we'll call her Maria. She was stuck in a toxic relationship, full of shame and self-doubt. She cried in class, flinched at contact, and hid behind her hair. But she never quit. Slowly, she reclaimed her voice. She earned her Black Belt, left the relationship, and became a role model.

Then there was Angela, a single mom with two young kids and no confidence. She barely spoke at first. But something in her spirit said "enough." She trained like her life depended on it—because it did. She found her strength, her power, and her joy.

They didn't just say, "I want a better life."
They *trained* for it. They *lived* it.
That's what amends in action looks like.

The Warrior's Code

A real warrior doesn't run from mistakes—he learns from them.
He doesn't deny his past—he transforms it.
He builds from the ashes.

I will fight the dream-stealers.
I will not surrender to shame or fear.
I will give, serve, and grow—daily.

"Tell me I can't? I'll show you I will.
Tell me it's impossible? I'll make it inevitable."

"Happiness is not found in pleasure, but in the development of reason and the adjustment of conduct to principles."
- Arnold Bennett

The Power of Amends

This chapter isn't about guilt - it's about growth.

It's about turning pain into purpose.
It's about showing up differently.
It's about living in a way that says:
"I remember who I was—and I'm committed to who I am becoming."

That's the Black Belt path.
That's recovery.
That's being Unshakeable.

Unshakeable Reminder -

Every mistake is a lesson. Every apology is a promise. And every day is a chance to live that promise out loud.
Stay teachable. Stay humble. Keep showing up.

"Grudges are heavy, but bridges are strong.
One keeps you stuck, the other moves you forward."
- Brad Wenneberg, Shihan

Chapter 12 - Palms Up

"The greatest gift you can give someone is the openness of your heart."
- Anonymous

For much of my early life, I didn't realize I was pushing people away with the very hands that longed to be held.
The lesson? **Healing begins when we turn our palms up.**

Have you ever felt like people were repelled by you? That no one seemed to notice you, connect with you, or want to be your friend?
I sure have.

For a long time, I didn't understand why. Now, looking back, I realize that much of it was of my own making. The programming I received growing up taught me that connection meant disappointment, and people always left. So, I kept everyone at arm's length—emotionally and sometimes even physically.

Walls and Wounds

During my police academy interview, the officer reviewing my background said,
"Brad, we discovered that you've lived in 21 different homes, changed schools over six times, and never stayed in one place more than two years. Do you think that kind of instability affected you psychologically?"

I was 21. "Of course not," I said.
What did I know?

What I didn't realize was how deeply my childhood had shaped me.
I had learned not to trust, not to connect, not to get involved.
People leave. That was the unspoken rule.

So, I built walls. I guarded myself. And I lived behind those walls for many years.

I see it in the dojo, too. A new student steps onto the mat unsure of themselves with their arms crossed, head down, back turned during partner work. They don't know it, but their body is saying, *stay away.*

Then comes that first moment of breakthrough—when they relax their arms, open their hands, and bow from the heart. That's when the real training begins.
Not just technique... but trust.

My stepdad and mom never showed affection toward each other. They lived like roommates. I never once heard "I love you." I never saw them hug. No tenderness.

No warmth. Just survival - and a lot of yelling.
My mom was dominant; my stepdad faded into the background.
I never saw a loving marriage modeled.

So, when I got married at 19, I had no clue how to be emotionally intimate.
My wife needed hugs, closeness, affection.

And I, metaphorically and literally, held out my hands—palms down—like a stop sign: **stay back**.

I was connected when I wanted sex, but otherwise I kept a distance. That became a painful theme in my life.
I longed to belong—but I was terrified. That little boy inside me had been hurt too many times.
So I built a wall and stood behind it, arms outstretched, palms down.

And then I'd wondered: *Why doesn't anyone like me? Why won't they approach me? What's wrong with me?*

The truth? I was still a scared little boy trying to pretend I was a man.

Enter the Bottle

Then... I found alcohol.

Suddenly, I was Taller. Smarter. Cooler. No more pimples. I could talk to girls. I felt alive—at least for a while.

Alcohol gave me permission to be carefree. I thought I'd found the cure.
But the cure became the poison.

What began as a solution turned into a disease.
I didn't just have childhood wounds anymore—I now had an addiction on top of them.
I withdrew. I isolated. I got sicker in mind, body, and spirit.

(We'll get more into that part of the story in later chapters.)

Palms Down in the Rooms

When I started going to AA meetings, I noticed something that hurt:
People didn't seem to want to talk to me.
No one shook my hand. No one approached me. I felt invisible—and angry about it.

One day, I shared that frustration with a guy after the meeting.

He looked at me and said,
"Brad, people don't approach you because you send out a signal that says, 'Stay away.' You literally hold your hands out like this—palms down—as if to say, 'Don't come any closer.' It's not them. It's you."

Then he added something that rocked me:
"When you learn to let people in—when you can hold your hands out with palms up—you'll start to see a change.
People want to know you, Brad. But you've got to let them in."

Turning My Hands—and Heart

That moment changed everything.

I realized I was repelling people without even meaning to.
I wanted connection but didn't know how to invite it in.
I had been protecting myself for so long that I didn't know how to surrender, how to trust, how to receive.

So, I changed.

I started practicing a new posture—not just with my body, but with my spirit.
Palms up. Open. Willing. Ready to connect.

It wasn't easy. Old habits die hard.
But with time, tools, and truth—many of which I share throughout this book—I began to heal.

I started to believe I was worth knowing.
I learned to let others in.
Slowly, the world responded—not with rejection, but with welcome.

"Vulnerability is not winning or losing; it's having the courage to show up and be seen."
- Brené Brown

The Black Belt Way

A Black Belt doesn't just know how to defend—they know when to open up.

A fist must close to strike, but a hand must open to heal.
Both are part of the martial artist's journey.

I used to think strength meant never needing anyone. That was ego.
I've come to believe that one of the highest Black Belt Basics is this:
Be strong enough to stay open.

Black Belts serve. They connect. They bow with presence.
Their *gi* may be pressed, their technique sharp—but their real power comes from how they treat others.
From how they show up - with their palms up.

Unshakeable Reminder -

Are your hands out, palms down—pushing people away—or open, palms up, inviting them in?

Practice the posture of palms up.

Connection begins when we let go of fear and let others come close.

Black Belt Basics aren't just drills and discipline.
They're how we show up—with presence, humility, and open hands.

"Surrender isn't weakness.
It's the doorway to deeper strength."
- Brad Wenneberg, Shihan

Chapter 13 - Face the Fear, Find the Freedom

"You gain strength, courage, and confidence by every experience in which you really stop to look fear in the face."
— Eleanor Roosevelt

Fear can be a teacher—or a tyrant.
For many years, I let it be the latter.
Fear kept me from speaking up when I should have. Fear kept me in toxic patterns. Fear whispered lies like, “You’re not enough,” “You’re not ready,” and worst of all, “You’re alone.” For too long, I believed it.

In martial arts, fear shows up the moment we step onto the mat. Especially in sparring—your heart races, your breath shortens, your mind fills with doubt.
But you step forward anyway. You bow. You breathe. You engage.
That’s the lesson:
Fear doesn’t mean stopping. It means focus.

When I began my sobriety journey, fear screamed in my ear.
It told me I couldn’t live without the crutch. That I’d fail. That I’d disappoint everyone—again. It convinced me I was broken, beyond repair. In those early days, it took everything I had to sit still, stay sober, and face myself.
I had to make a choice:

Would I let fear keep me sick—or would I fight for my life?

Recovery didn't eliminate fear. It exposed it. And then it gave me tools to walk through it. Step by step. Meeting by meeting. Truth by truth.
The truth is, **everyone feels fear**—Black Belts, CEOs, pastors, parents, teenagers, fire fighters, police officers, addicts in early recovery. Me. You. All of us.

Not everyone faces it.
Even fewer walk through it.

"Feel the fear and do it anyway."
- Susan Jeffers

Sometimes fear is loud and obvious—like stepping into a ring. Other times, it's quiet and sneaky—like the fear of success, or of disappointing someone you love. But either way, fear loses its grip when we move toward it instead of running from it.

The Day I Froze

Years ago, during my law enforcement days, I was first on the scene to a violent domestic call. I drew my weapon and approached the doorway. My training told me to move—but my body wouldn't budge. I froze.

In that brief but terrifying moment, I realized something crucial:
Fear isn't weakness, it's information.
And what you do next determines who you become.

What got me moving wasn't bravado. It was breathing. Training. A deep inner voice that said, *"You know what to do—now take the step."*

That moment taught me more about courage than any classroom ever could.

Fear as a Compass

Fear isn't always the enemy. Sometimes it's the guide.
It shows up right before the breakthrough. It visits when we're about to level up. If we're listening, it can point us to the very place that needs healing or growth.

Fear is a door. Knock on it. Then walk through.
Your future self is waiting on the other side.

Mia and the Board

One of our students—a quiet girl named Mia—stood frozen in front of the board she needed to break at her belt test. Her lip trembled. Her hands shook. Parents were watching. Tears welled in her eyes.

We waited.

Then, she looked over at me. I nodded once. She took a deep breath, kiai'd loud enough to rattle the mirrors, and struck.

The board shattered.
So did the lie in her head that said, "I can't."

Fear didn't disappear. But it lost its hold.
And a warrior stepped forward.

Fear, Faith, and the Next Step

We hear it in the rooms and in whispers from mentors:

FEAR = False Evidence Appearing Real.

Fear feeds on projection. On worst-case scenarios. On the illusion of control.

Faith lives in the present.

It reminds us that we don't need to see the whole staircase; we just need to take the next right step.

Someone once told me in recovery:

"Fear is none of your business. That's God's business. Your business is to do the next indicated thing."

At first, I didn't understand. But over time, that truth became one of the pillars of my life.
Fear is often a sign that I've left the present. Left faith. Left humility.

When I look back, every crossroads—every blessing, every setback, every hard detour—was leading me right here. Even the heartbreaks had hidden lessons. The doors that slammed shut were often divine redirections.

So, what helps me stay grounded when fear creeps in?

- **Prayer -** I don't have to figure it all out. I can hand it over to my Higher Power.
- **Mentorship -** Someone wiser walked this road before— I can ask for help.

- **Meditation -** Slow the noise. Tune in to truth.
- **Rituals -** Little daily anchors that make me feel spiritually cozy—like reading morning affirmations, breathing, or making my bed.
- **The next indicated thing -** Don't over think. Just move.

Sometimes courage doesn't look like charging a mountain. Sometimes it looks like staying sober for one more hour. Sometimes it looks like telling the truth in a tough conversation. Sometimes it's just **getting out of bed and showing up anyway.**

Black Belt Basics for Facing Fear

So how do we train to face fear?

- **We show up scared.** Not perfect. Not fearless. Just willing.
- **We breathe.** Fear shortens breath. Warriors deepen it.
- **We speak truth.** Whether in AA, the dojo, or our relationships, truth disarms fear.
- **We lean on others.** Courage is contagious. So is surrender.
- **We remember what matters.** Fear fades when purpose grows louder.

I've faced the fear of relapses. The fear of losing everything. The fear of failing my family.

I've feared cancer, bankruptcy, shame, and even dying alone. And here's what I've learned:

Most of what I feared never actually happened.
What did happen? I survived it. I grew from it.
And I was never as alone as fear made me feel.
Courage isn't the absence of fear.
It's the decision that something else matters more.

Unshakeable Reminder -

Fear visits everyone—but it doesn't have to live with us.
Let's pause and ask:
What fear have we let sit in the driver's seat for too long?

Today is a good day to reclaim the wheel.
Courage begins with one bold step forward.

"The mat doesn't care how scared you are—it only asks, 'Will you take the step?'"
- Brad Wenneberg, Shihan

"Fear may visit, but it doesn't get to unpack. Faith lives here now."
- Erica Campbell

Chapter 14 - The Courage to Ask for Help

"Change begins when honesty meets action."
- Brad Wenneberg, Shihan

The Archer's Bow

A student admired the bows hung in the master's hall.
"I've studied every scroll on archery," he said. "Surely I am ready."

The master placed a bow in his hands.
"Then draw."

The student strained and failed. His arms shook. His face flushed.

The master smiled. "Knowledge fills the mind. Action strengthens the muscle. Without both, no arrow will fly."

I thought of this lesson when I met Valerie, a woman who had read the books, joined the programs, and prayed for change—but hadn't yet found the strength to draw her own bow.

She was sad. Depressed. Completely bankrupt—body, mind, and spirit. You could hear it in her voice and see it in her posture. She was stuck in a painful marriage, a smoker, severely overweight, and buried under years of hopelessness.

Then one day, she said the magic words:
"I need help."

Those three words changed everything.

When I asked what she had tried, she listed it all: gyms, trainers, hypnosis, diets, even a church group. But her eyes welled with tears as she cried, "Nothing works. It's useless. I'm a loser. Can you help me?"

I told her gently, "Valerie, I can't fix your life. But I can share what worked for me. If anything I say makes sense, I pray it gives you direction—and a little hope."

Hope + Action

There's a myth that thinking positive alone will fix our lives; but attitude by itself isn't enough.

Your self-talk matters.

- **If we think we will fail, we probably will.**
- **If we think about prosperity, we invite good things.**

However, thinking is only the beginning. What we think shapes what we do—and what we do shapes who we become.

Valerie didn't need another program. She needed a decision. She didn't need another system. She needed consistent and persistent action.

Wishing doesn't change us. Training does.

My Own Lesson

Years ago, I was bankrupt—financially, emotionally, physically, spiritually. I prayed. I read books. I told myself it would get better. But nothing changed until I actually did.

I didn't dabble. I committed.
I didn't just hope. I trained.
I didn't rely on luck. I acted.
I didn't do it part-time. I did it consistently and persistently.

With mentors and a recovery group, I learned this: change doesn't come from trying harder. It comes from doing differently.

From Victim to Warrior

Programs don't work *for* us. That gym won't lift the weights. That mentor won't walk the steps. That prayer won't change the habits we refuse to change.

It doesn't matter if you're a woman or a man, an adult or a child—the principle is the same. Transformation requires action.

We can't expect long-term change from short-term effort. Two months of part-time effort won't undo twenty years of dysfunction.

Valerie didn't need another treadmill. She needed to remember what it felt like to stand tall. She wasn't broken. She wasn't a loser. She was a warrior in training.

Warrior Wisdom from the Mat

In the dojo, we teach that how you walk can prevent an attack before it begins. Posture. Presence. Confidence. That applies to everyone. Walk like a victim, and you may be treated like one. Walk like a warrior—with strength, awareness, and dignity—and many challenges back down before they even begin.

Some days, you won't feel strong. So what do you do? You act strong. You carry yourself like a warrior until your spirit catches up with your stance.

That's not faking it - that's training it.

One Final Hug

One of my mentors in AA, facing terminal bone cancer, taught me this truth. Frail and dying, he smiled and said, "I've learned to live with dignity and gratitude. Now I'm learning to die the same way."

He reminded me—and Valerie—that we act our way into better living. We serve our way into deeper meaning. We walk like the warrior we are becoming.

Closing Echo

In the end, Valerie —and all of us—must learn the same truth the young archer faced:
No scroll, no teacher, no prayer alone can release the arrow.

The bow only bends when we put our hands on it.
The arrow only flies when we draw and release.
And life only transforms when we take the next step with courage.

Unshakeable Reminder -

Stop hoping for change. Start training for it, and be consistent long term.
Life doesn't shift with another book, another app, another plan.

It changes when we take consistent, focused, humble action—especially when we don't feel like it.

"We face things in life we can't fix, fight, or figure out.
True peace begins the moment we say three magical words:
'I need help.'"
- Sadhguru

Chapter 15 - The Words That Set Me Free

"When I started telling myself the truth, my healing began."
- Brad Wenneberg, Shihan

My story isn't unique. It's not special.
It's just... mine.

One of the things I've always appreciated about Alcoholics Anonymous is that we don't give advice or tell others what to do.

We share -
What it was like.
What happened.
And what it's like today.

So this isn't a sermon. This is me, sharing what I went through—what I did to repair and heal. And hopefully, somewhere in these pages, you'll find something that gives you hope.

Music, Laughter, and Then the Shouting

From my earliest memories, my childhood home was filled with music and energy. My brother Ross played the drums—really played—and even cut records that still get radio play. My older sister Bonnie was a dazzling dancer, winning contests and owning any dance floor she touched. My mom had a lovely voice and could whistle like a champ.

Ross would drum, Bonnie would dance, and Mom would sing—all while I watched, trying to keep up. It was loud, chaotic fun.

It felt like family.
It felt normal.

My stepdad Hugh worked selling wine in Los Angeles. We had a stable, middle-class life—until he lost his job at 55.
Suddenly, he couldn't find work because of his age. We lost the house. Finances crumbled. We began moving from place to place—sometimes three times on the same block. Once, we even moved back into a house we'd already lived in.

That's when the family started to break down.
The arguments turned louder. The violence more frequent.
The words hurled at us—*stupid, ugly, failure*—became the soundtrack of my fear.

I'd curl up in a corner, hands over my ears, trying to drown out the shouting and rage.
One by one, my siblings were pushed out.
That's when I believe my self-worth was shattered.

My Sister's Illness

As if the stress wasn't enough, our family was stretched even further by my younger sister's mysterious illness.

Without warning, she would fall into convulsions and stop breathing.

I watched in terror as my mother or sister threw her into an ice-cold bathtub until the ambulance arrived. I was ten years old—scared, confused, and overwhelmed by the chaos around me.

Eventually, doctors discovered she had a failing kidney valve. She was one of the first to receive a valve replacement.
Thank God—it worked.
But that trauma was another weight on our already-fractured home.
We weren't just fighting to survive financially—we were fighting for sanity.

Northbound and Downhill

When doctors advised that my mom's emphysema required cleaner air, we moved north to a place a bit east of San Francisco. I was 15, yanked from Southern California where I had friends, identity, and hope.

Up north, I was miserable.

My mother's illness got worse. Gasping for air, she became unpredictable—sometimes loving, often violent. I did my best to care for her. We'd watch Johnny Carson and laugh—tiny echoes of a happier time. But those nights were the exception, not the rule.

I became that scared little boy again, coiled in the corner, whispering a vow to myself:
"I will never be like this."

Addiction Finds Me

Addiction runs deep in my family—alcohol, pills, nicotine.
I found out I wasn't immune at 16.

My brother bought my friends and I a bottle of Southern Comfort Whiskey. That night, after just one drink, I locked myself in the bathroom and drank the whole thing.

They dumped me on the living room floor and left.
I'm told I crawled into bed with my younger sister and promptly vomited all over her.
I woke up around 4 p.m. the next day with my mother at the foot of the bed.

She looked down at me and said:
"You look just like your drunken father. Alcohol killed him—and it will kill you too."

I promised, "Mom, I'll never drink again."

I meant it.

At 7 p.m., I told her I needed fresh air.
I walked to a liquor store, found a guy to buy me vodka; and by 7:30, I was drunk again.

That was the beginning of my alcoholic journey.

Mom's Final Words

Years later, when Mom was nearing the end of her life, she asked if my wife and I would raise my 14-year-old brother.

I said yes.

Then she looked at me—really looked at me—and spoke the most important words I've ever heard:

"Brad, my son, I may have screwed you up; but it's up to you to fix it."

That sentence changed everything.

Those words allowed me to forgive.
To stop blaming.
To take responsibility.
To start healing.

They didn't just give me permission.
They gave me power.
Power to change my story.

The Bamboo Cutter's Son
(*Adapted from Japanese folklore*)

Long ago in Japan, a bamboo cutter found a crying child abandoned in the forest. He raised the boy as his own, but as the child grew, he became bitter. He blamed his unknown parents, the villagers, even his adoptive father for his pain.

One day, after another angry outburst, the old man handed him a stalk of bamboo.

"Split it," he said.
The boy did.

"Now mend it."

"I can't," the boy said.

"No one can," replied the old man. "That's the way with blame—it cuts, but cannot mend. However, if you grow your own bamboo, tend your own grove, shape your own future—then you can build something strong."

From that day on, the boy stopped blaming.
And started building.

Unshakeable Reminder -

We don't choose how our story begins.
But we do choose how it continues.

The Warrior doesn't stay stuck in the pain of the past—
He turns it into purpose.

We all inherit broken bamboo—
But the Warrior grows his own grove.

Healing begins the moment we stop pointing fingers
and start planting roots.

What part of your story still holds pain—and are you ready to grow your own grove from it?
Write one thing you're ready to stop blaming... and one thing you're ready to start building.

"It's better to be a warrior in a garden,
than a gardener in a war,"
- Japanese proverb

"The only real battle in life is between hanging on and letting go."
- Shannon L. Alder

Chapter 16 - The Day the Fog Lifted

"Pain is real. So is hope!"
- Anne-Marie Lockmyer

Before I continue this chapter, I want to make one thing clear.
I am not a doctor. I'm not a psychiatrist, therapist, or psychologist.
But I am a survivor. A warrior.
What I can offer you is the truth of my own journey with mental illness.
If it resonates with you, I hope it helps. If it doesn't apply to your life directly, there's a good chance someone close to you is walking through something similar. Keep reading for them.

In the year 2000, I attended a Thursday night AA meeting. This wasn't just any meeting. It was my home group. I've been going for over 20 years. I knew the people. I knew the rhythm.

That night, I showed up with three months sobriety, again... and completely in despair.

Something was wrong.
I had done everything AA had taught me, worked the steps, called my sponsor, read the literature, served others—and yet I felt worse, not better.
Shaky. Vulnerable. Afraid.

At the break, I walked up to my sponsor, Mike, and said, "I'm not okay."
I told him everything I had been doing, and how none of it was

helping. I told him I wanted to disappear.
Mike put his hand on my shoulder and said, "AA is powerful. But some of us need more help. You need more help. And you need to go find it."

We walked back into the meeting, and something miraculous happened.
A man I had never seen before—and have never seen since—sat down beside me and said, "Excuse me. I heard you during the break."
He handed me a business card.
It was for a psychiatrist.
He said, "Call this number in the morning."
And that was it. He left.

I don't remember what I shared during the second half of that meeting, but I remember gripping that card like it was a lifeline. And it was.

Intervention and Light

Divine intervention? I believe so.

The next morning, I dialed the number.
"Is this Brad?" the man on the line asked.
"Yes."
"I'd like you and your wife to come in today at 2:00 PM. Bring an overnight bag."

Later that morning, we discovered that the doctor I was about to see was California's lead psychiatrist specializing in depression.

Sure, I'd felt a little off before. Down. Tired. Sad.
But I thought, *it'll pass. Everyone gets blue now and then.*

At 2:00 PM sharp, Bonnie and I walked into his office—inside a nearby hospital.
We were ushered into a private room.
And for the first time in a long time...
I felt a glimmer of hope.

The doctor leaned forward, locked eyes with me, and said in a calm, unwavering voice:
"Brad, you are in a serious and dangerous state of mind; and without proper treatment, I believe you will go back to where you were—only this time, worse."

He explained that I needed a full, complete medical diagnosis before it was too late.
I asked him who was the man at the meeting—the one who gave me his card.
The doctor looked at me and said, "I have no idea who you're talking about."

I was admitted for inpatient evaluation—no timeline.
"As long as it takes," he said.

They combed through my entire life:
My childhood medical records. My school behavior. My family history. My years of emotional instability. My adult highs and lows.

I had always assumed I was simply "a little depressed." I had even been on a low dose of antidepressants.

But nothing ever changed—because nothing had been properly diagnosed.

When it came time to hear the results, Bonnie and I sat down in his office again.
The psychiatrist didn't sugarcoat it:

"You're not just depressed, Brad.
You have bipolar disorder; and based on your symptoms and history—dangerous bipolar." The medication I'd been taking wasn't helping. In fact, it was making my condition worse.

He laid out the symptoms like a blueprint of my life:

- Sadness without cause
- Emotional chaos
- A sense of doom
- Trouble sleeping
- Constant noise in my head
- Dreading the mornings
- Explosive anger or deep despair without warning
- Wild decisions during manic states—like buying a business on a whim that cost us over $250,000

Then he said something that humbled me deeply:
"Brad, you've been self-medicating for years—trying to manage your illness through alcohol.
That doesn't mean you're not an alcoholic. That disease is separate, inherited, and would have existed anyway.

But the bipolar disorder magnified it—and made it even more dangerous."

He gave me a 'corrected' prescription and within a week, I could feel the shift.

Then one morning, I opened my eyes and called Bonnie.
"Bonnie... the world is in color.
Is this what it's suppose to feel like?"
She smiled and said, "Yes, my love."
And then she hugged me like never before.

That was over two decades ago.

Since then, through careful adjustments and ongoing treatment, my bipolar symptoms have been minimal. I still take my medication.

And yes, from time to time, the shadows of depression creep back in.

However, I've found something powerful: **acceptance**.
And more than that, I've built a blueprint:
Rituals. Support. Discipline. Self-awareness. And a warrior's commitment to truth.

Just like martial arts, just like sobriety, this life is not about perfection.
It's about practice.
It's about presence.
It's about building something that holds—even when the wind howls.

A Note on Clinical Depression

Some people go through a tough week, feel down for a while, and then bounce back. That's part of being human.
Clinical depression is something different.

It's not just feeling sad. It's a diagnosable medical condition—one that impacts brain chemistry, energy, focus, sleep, and even decision-making. It doesn't go away just because we "try harder" or "think positive."

It must be professionally diagnosed.
That's a key part of the journey that I wish more people understood. I didn't just wake up one day and figure it out—I had to get real help. I had to be evaluated, treated, and supported over time. That's not weakness. That's wisdom.

There is no shame in needing help. There is only danger in not getting it.

If someone you care about has been in a deep fog for weeks or months, encourage them to get assessed by a specifically-trained doctor in mental illness. Medication isn't always the answer—but when it is, it can save lives.

Let's Talk About Anxiety

Anxiety is like trying to drive with the parking brake on.
You can still move, but it's exhausting. It makes everything harder.

Some days, I feel anxious for no apparent reason. Heart pounding. Mind racing.

Other days, it's quiet—but always there, humming beneath the surface.

Anxiety tells lies:
That the worst is about to happen.
That you're unsafe.
That you can't handle what's next.

What has helped?

- **Acceptance.** I stopped trying to "fight" anxiety and learned to recognize it with compassion.
- **Mindfulness.** Breathing. Grounding. Noticing the moment I'm in—not the one I'm afraid is coming.
- **Structure.** Routines help. Rituals help.
- **Service.** Helping someone else resets my brain like nothing else.

I used to think peace came from the absence of anxiety.
Now I know it comes from how I respond when it shows up.

Let's Talk About OCD (Obsessive-compulsive disorder)

This one is less talked about—but it showed up in my life in subtle (and sometimes not-so-subtle) ways.
I didn't know what to call it at first. But over the years of treatment and healing, I've come to recognize it for what it is: OCD-like patterns that sneak in and try to take over.

Here are a few:

- Straightening pictures obsessively
- Topping off my gas tank only at even dollar amounts
- Putting things in perfect order—even if it takes ten extra minutes

I once asked my psychiatrist about it. He grinned and said,
"At least you're not robbing banks."
We laughed. And that helped.

OCD tendencies don't make me broken. They make me human.
And like with anxiety, acceptance is key.

I've learned not to beat myself up when the patterns appear.
I use the same **Unshakeable** principles that saved me from alcohol and depression:

- **Awareness**
- **Ritual**
- **Reframing**
- **Surrender**

This Is Not About Perfection

Recovery isn't about eliminating every problem.
It's about building a life that works even when the problems come.
It's about living with presence and compassion, especially for yourself.

Mental illness does not disqualify you from a good life.
It means you walk with different challenges.
But you still walk—with purpose, and with strength.

Unshakeable Reminder -

Mental health isn't a weakness. It's part of the warrior's path. Honor it. Own it. And build your daily practice around truth—not fear.

"We don't need to be fixed. We need to become Unshakeable by the tools to be found in truth, in consistency, in grace, and sometimes... in medicine."

- Brad Wenneberg, Shihan
(adapted from Tony Robbins)

Chapter 17 - Living Two Lives in One Lifetime

"True strength is not found in the strike — it's in the surrender (letting go of the ego, resistance, and the need to control).
- Adapted from martial arts philosophy

Let's talk about present-day Brad.

I've been married since 1973 to the love of my life. We have two wonderful children, five amazing grandchildren, and we've built the home of our dreams. We've traveled the world, and we own one of the largest and most successful karate schools in North America, with over 1,000 students. We're financially free. And above all — I've been sober since February 12, 2000.

You might be wondering, "Why share all this?"

Because what you see now isn't the whole story. I've lived two completely different lives in one lifetime — the man I was, and the man I am today. A story of brokenness and rebuilding. Addiction and recovery. Darkness and light.

Now, maybe you're thinking, *"This chapter isn't for me."* But let me gently challenge that. Maybe you're not an alcoholic or drug addict — and that's great. But I'd bet you have someone in your life who is. A spouse. A child. A sibling. A coworker. A neighbor.

This disease doesn't play favorites — it finds its way into all our lives.
If you know and care about someone who suffers... you suffer too.
If that's you, this chapter is for you.

The Descent

It was the summer of 1969 when I had my first real drink. From the very first sip, something clicked — or maybe, unclicked. I wanted more. One drink turned into ten. One moment of fun turned into years of destruction.

Back then, I was a standout on the high school track team — the 800-meters was my event. That year at the state meet, instead of preparing like a champion, I was drinking in the stands. Loud. Belligerent. Embarrassing. I raised my beer in the air and shouted that the whole thing was "a joke." I heckled the race I was supposed to win.

The winner that day in that event ran five seconds slower than my worst time. I believe I would have won again — if only.

At the varsity awards ceremony, my name wasn't called. I had been a school champion for three years, and in my mind, I had earned that letter. How dare they leave me out?

After the ceremony, my coach looked me in the eye and said words I'll never forget:

"Brad, you let the school down. You let the team down. You let me down... but mostly, you let yourself down."

Then he turned and walked away.

I didn't feel remorse. I felt rage. I told myself I was the victim. But the truth lingered.

Years later, when I got sober and began working the steps to sobriety, I was driven to make amends. One of the letters I wrote was to my high school. I owned it. I apologized for my behavior that night — for dishonoring the team and letting my ego lead the way.

Two weeks later, an envelope arrived in the mail.

No note. No explanation.
Just my varsity letter — the one I never received back then.

A moment of grace.
A quiet redemption.
A reminder that healing is always possible... if we're willing to take the first step.

The Spiral

As a young police officer, I became a functioning drunk. I showed up. I got the job done. But inside, the disease was quietly tightening its grip.

Bonnie, my wife, bore the brunt of it. She worked full-time, covered for me, and still lived in fear. I never physically hurt her, but the verbal rage, the unpredictability; the blackout nights... they left scars.

After an injury forced me into medical retirement, I spiraled. My career was over. My purpose? Gone. I sat at home, drinking all day, growing a long, unkempt beard, sinking deeper into despair while Bonnie fought to keep our lives from falling apart.

I lied to my psychologist. I lied to Bonnie. And I lied to myself.

Until one day, Marv — my therapist — ripped up my payment to him in the middle of a session.

"Brad," he said, "You're nothing more than a drunk. I can't help you until you're ready to get sober. Go to an AA meeting. Then come back."

"The chains of addiction are too weak to feel until they are too strong to break — unless you ask for help."
- adapted from Samuel Johnson

The First Step

That night in 1978, when I walked into my first AA meeting, I was terrified.
But what I saw shocked me even more than the fear — people were laughing. Hugging. Smiling. Genuinely happy.

I thought, *They must be loaded... no one has that much fun sober.*

But they weren't. They were clean. And they had something I desperately wanted: Freedom. Peace. Joy.
I wish I could tell you I got sober that night. I didn't.

I kept going to meetings but kept drinking too, on and off.
It wasn't until 1984 that I truly got sober for the first time.

That's when I began to understand the nature of addiction:
It's not a lack of willpower.
It's twofold — a physical allergy (once I start, I can't stop) and a

mental obsession (once I stop, I can't stop thinking about starting again).
That's the trap.

I admitted I was powerless. I got a sponsor. I did the work.
And I stayed sober... for a while.

The Relapse Years

Here's the truth: My sobriety date isn't 1984. It's February 12, 2000.

Because along the way, I got cocky. I stopped going to meetings. I stopped doing the daily disciplines. I believed the lie: *I got this.*

In 1992, I drank again. Badly. I nearly died.
I got sober.
Then I relapsed again in 1996.
It took four more years of pain, denial, of seeking professional mental medical help, and defeat before I finally surrendered — for good.

The Flatbed Truck

Some stories stick with you like broken glass.

One night, around 3 AM, I was driving home from Los Angeles to Orange Co. Drunk.
When I was just about home, I plowed into the back of a flatbed truck. The impact was deafening. The windshield shattered, slicing the side of my head wide open.

I crawled out of the car, blood gushing down my face, and dropped to my knees in the middle of the road. I tilted my head to the sky and begged:
"God, please... make this a dream."
I opened my eyes.
It wasn't.

A week later, I was driving again — beer between my legs.
It's a miracle I didn't kill someone — or myself.

That's addiction.
Cunning. Baffling. Powerful.
Without help... it's too much for us.

The Mirror

Finally, it wasn't the crashes.
It wasn't the shouting.
It wasn't even the pain that I caused others.

It was a quiet moment. Alone.

I looked in the bathroom mirror — really looked — and saw what others had seen for years: A broken man. Hollow eyes. Bloated face. Spirit defeated.

I didn't recognize him.
I hated him.

That mirror didn't just reflect a man — it revealed a battlefield.
And I was losing.

That's when the armor cracked. That's when the real work began.

The Climb Back

Since 2000, I've been sober. One day at a time.
Some days are loud. Some are quiet. Some are hard. But none are hopeless.

I show up. I call my sponsor. I stay connected. I help others. I do the work.

Bonnie didn't trust me right away — nor should she have.
But little by little, I showed up. I became the man she deserved.
Not perfect — just present.

The life I live today — this beautiful, unshakeable life — is built on the foundation of surrender.

I've lived two lives in one lifetime.
Although I carry the scars of the first, I wouldn't trade it because of the lessons learned, the experiences received, and the second amazing purposeful life that it has given me.

Black Belt Basics and Recovery

Sobriety and martial arts share the same DNA:

- **Discipline:** Daily habits. Consistent training. Humility before ego.
- **Mentorship:** Sponsors and Senseis — both guide us back to center.
- **Relapse and Regression:** Stop practicing the basics… and you backslide.

- **Surrender:** Not weakness — wisdom. Letting go is the beginning of power.

Both paths require commitment.
Both demand honesty.
Both... save lives.

Unshakeable Reminder -

You can live two lives in one lifetime.
Choose the one built on truth, discipline, and surrender.
And never walk it alone.

"There is no fast-forward button on transformation.
The Unshakeable warrior's path is not rushed - it's walked one step at a time
with faith, focus, and consistency."
- Brad Wenneberg, Shihan

Chapter 18 - If You Can Look Up, You Can Get Up

"It's not whether you get knocked down;
it's whether you get up."
— Vince Lombardi

His name is Jeremy

His mom brought him into my studio at the ripe old age of six. She sat with tears in her eyes and told me, "He has no confidence. No self-esteem. He won't talk much, won't play on his own, and struggles to connect with other kids." She was desperate. She just wanted her son to feel okay in his own skin.

The missing piece? Jeremy was nearly completely deaf. That explained a lot—but it didn't define him. Not in my dojo.

I got down on one knee, looked Jeremy in the eye, and asked him: "Are you ready and willing to do whatever it takes to feel better?" He looked back and answered, loud and clear:
"Yes, sir."

And so began the journey.

Here's the truth: We can't teach confidence. We can't hand someone self-esteem. It must be developed. It must be earned—through failure, success, sweat, tears, and resilience.

I designed his journey to include both. I put him in situations where he would fail and learn to get back up. I gave him moments where he could win and feel the joy of his own progress.

I surrounded him with structure, love, and belief. And over time, Jeremy didn't just change—he blossomed.

Confidence comes from action

Confidence comes from stepping into discomfort, again and again, and learning, "I can do this."
It's not instant. It's not easy. It's earned.

Jeremy didn't become confident because he was told to.
He became confident because he lived it, he discovered it.
Because he showed up.
One action step at a time.
One "Yes Sir" at a time.

That quiet, insecure six-year-old is now in his forties. He's traveled the world, trained in multiple martial arts, and holds a high-ranking Black Belt. Through the very plan we created together, he learned how to teach, how to speak, and how to command a room.

Jeremy has been a master instructor in my school for decades now. He's earned the respect of thousands—on and off the mat. He is an honored friend, a true warrior, and a living reminder of what happens when someone decides to get up, keep the faith, and take that next action step.

Your miracle is waiting to bloom.

A Warrior's Reflection

One of the most important lessons I have ever learned came from a simple phrase I heard early in recovery:

Unshakeable

"If you can look up, you can get up."
- Les Brown

It stuck with me—not just because it was catchy, but because it was true.
Life has knocked me down more than once. I've faced addiction, depression, cancer, and self-doubt. I've laid flat—physically, emotionally, and spiritually. But every time, there was a spark. A whisper inside that said:
Look up.

When I did—when I shifted my gaze from the problem to the possibility, from the shame to the solution—I found the strength to rise.

In the dojo, students stumble. They fall in kata, they lose in sparring, they forget forms. But the Black Belt mindset isn't about never falling—it's about always getting back up. Every belt earned is a story of resilience.

This chapter is a reminder:
You will fall.
You will fail.
You will struggle.
But you are not alone.
And the power to rise is already within you.
So, when you hit the mat—even when it's hard—don't stay down.
Take a breath. Look up. And get up.
Because your next victory begins the moment you decide not to quit.

"Rock bottom became the solid foundation
on which I rebuilt my life."
- J.K. Rowling

Unshakeable Reminder -

Falling isn't abject failure—it's feedback.
What matters is that we rise, even if it's slow, even if it's messy.
Let's remember: Every setback holds the seed of a comeback.
Eyes up, heart open—let's get up and go again.

"The mat doesn't judge you for falling.
It invites you to rise again."
- Brad Wenneberg, Shihan

Chapter 19 - The Power of Mentorship

"The fastest way to reach your potential is to follow someone who's already walked the path — and then guide someone else along it."
- Brad Wenneberg, Shihan

Without mentorship, I would not be where I am today.

At ten years old, I took on my first job — a paper route. That first morning after having to wake up really early, I was already questioning my decision. Folding and rubber-banding each paper, loading them into the pouch on my bike, then riding the route for ninety minutes — it was not my idea of a dream job.

So, I went to my route manager and told him I was quitting because "the job sucked." He looked me in the eye and gave me advice that would change how I viewed leadership forever.

He said, "Be a manager to others - hire a crew, teach them the job, and you can sleep in."

I did just that. I hired three guys to fold, band, and deliver. Once a month, I collected the fees, paid them well, and still made a generous profit. That was my first taste of mentorship — guiding others and building something bigger than I could do alone.

Mentorship is the Way

Over the years, I found mentors in every major stage of my life. My college professor, who happened to be the police chief of a local city, mentored me through the process of joining the police department and even gave me a personal referral.

When I transitioned to a career into the insurance industry, my father-in-law, Leo, guided me. He became my business mentor and partner. I listened. I watched. We built a successful team together, helping many people secure important financial security.

In martial arts, I was blessed with incredible mentors — Shihan Gray, Sensei Ahrens, Andrew Wood, and Shihan Watson — each leaving a unique mark on my journey.

Rookie Lessons and Real Life

My first night as a police officer, I was assigned to a training officer. I had a college degree in police science and had just finished four months in the academy. I thought I was ready.

He looked at me and said, "Rookie, you don't know anything yet. You're about to enter the *real world*."
Later that night, we were dispatched to a domestic disturbance. As we approached the scene, a large man was shouting at his wife outside their home. Suddenly, he turned toward us, picked up a heavy chain, and raised it like a weapon.
And I froze.

When I became coherent again, the man was cuffed and on the ground.

Back in our patrol car, my training officer got nose-to-nose with me, and unloaded.

"You could've gotten us all killed," he yelled with many colorful words. "You froze. Book smarts mean nothing out here. You better start paying attention to **me**. You got a lot to learn and you better do it fast."
He punched my shoulder and said, "Get the report wrote, and let's get back on patrol."

That night changed everything for me. I realized that without a mentor, I wasn't just inexperienced - I was *at risk*.

In the Beginning

I have studied the martial arts since I was 19 years old and hold Black Belts in several different systems. However, opening a dojo was never on my radar. My transition to the martial arts business began in 1991.

One Sunday, after a two-day seminar about 'How to Be Successful in the Martial Arts Business' with Andrew Wood, he approached me with a question that would change my life.

"Are you happy working in insurance?" he asked.
I replied, "It's not exciting, but I'm making a good living."
Then he asked, "If you could do anything, what would it be?"
"Teach martial arts," I said.
His response was simple: "Then quit your insurance job and open your own dojo."

I went home that night, bursting with excitement, and announced to Bonnie, "I'm quitting insurance, and I'm going to open my own karate school."

After 'metaphorically' falling on the floor, she composed herself, looked straight into my eyes — no, into my heart — and listened as I shared my vision. When I was done, she said, "Okay - How can I help?"

The truth was that most karate studios closed within two years of when they opened; but I refused to even entertain the thought of failure. My purpose was clear: to be a Warrior — one who serves.

The next morning, I called Andrew and told him I was ready. I asked if he would mentor me. He asked if I was willing to do whatever it took to succeed.
"I'm all in," I told him.

For years, I called him daily. We talked about victories and setbacks, and he taught me everything from how to turn the key to open the door, to how to market, teach, and build a thriving community.

One morning shortly after opening our first dojo, he asked me what I was doing.
"Waiting for people to walk in," I said.
"Go get your white pages," he told me. (Obviously pre-internet, and we used a phone book!)
"What's the first name at the top of the list?"
I read it to him.
"Start with that one and start calling." He had given me a script. I had to start using it.

That week, I enrolled six new students.

He was my mentor, but I had to do the work — I had to listen, be honest, stay willing, and put in the effort. Within a few years, we had one of the most successful single-location martial arts schools in North America. Not because we were "so great," but because we created a system that welcomed everyone and gave them a place to grow.

In All My Affairs

Mentorship didn't stop with business. In Alcoholics Anonymous, I've had a sponsor — a mentor — since day one.
I've had a spiritual mentor, a business mentor, and a trusted confidant who knows me completely. Shihan Gray saw me at my worst and my best, guiding me as a life coach, a spiritual teacher, and a steady friend.

Since August 1985, I've met with one of my mentors every Thursday night without fail. Unless there's an emergency, I don't miss it. This isn't just something I did at the start. It's something I still do.

I believe this with my whole heart: Everything I have today is a direct result of being willing to have a mentor - willing to learn, to be honest, to be open-minded, and willing to do what those before me have done.

The Cup That Overflows

At every Black Belt ceremony, we hold a tea ritual. It's simple but symbolic.

Each of us pours tea into a small cup until it overflows. That overflow represents ego—the moment we become so full of ourselves that there's no room left to grow.

Then we pour some out.

This act reminds us to stay teachable. Stay open. Retain what we've learned, but empty our cups regularly so wisdom can enter. When you stop learning, you stop growing. When you stop growing, your belt color means nothing.

"Do not seek to follow in the footsteps of the men of old; seek what they sought."
- Matsuo Basho

The Master and the Young Warrior — A Parable

A young warrior once approached an old master and asked, "Master, how do I become wise and skilled like you?"

The master smiled and said, "Walk with me."

They walked into the forest where the path split in two directions — one smooth and straight, the other rocky and winding. "Which path do you choose?" the master asked.

"The smooth one, Master. It is easier and faster," the young warrior replied.

The master shook his head. "Then you will arrive quickly, but you will arrive small.
Walk the hard path — and I will walk with you. I will guide you around the dangers, teach you how to climb the rocks, and show

you where the streams run clear. You will arrive slower, but you will arrive stronger."

Mentorship is that guiding presence — walking with someone on the harder path so you arrive not just at the destination, but as the person you were meant to become.

Full Circle — Becoming the Mentor

One of my proudest moments was watching Jeremy, my young deaf student; grow from an unsure white belt into a confident master instructor. The same way my mentors believed in me, I believed in him. I pushed him when he wanted to quit, celebrated his victories, and helped him discover that his hearing impairment didn't limit his teaching ability — it enhanced it.

Then there was Sarah, a shy teenager whose parents hoped karate would give her confidence. Through years of encouragement, honest feedback, and shared sweat on the mat, she transformed into a leader who could command a room of students with the same presence my mentors taught me to carry.

In both cases, I realized I was simply passing forward what had been given to me — guidance, belief, and the push to step into a bigger life.

My claim to fame isn't my rank, my title, or even my business. It's having a purpose, a vision, and a dream — and being willing to do whatever it takes to carry that message into the future.

If I could name one force that's shaped my success more than anything else, it's this:

Mentorship.
Not luck, not raw talent, not even 'grit'.

It's been *people* - mentors - who walked before me, who saw things I couldn't, and who dared to tell me the truth.

Some taught by example, some by compassion, and some by giving me the sharp nudge I didn't want - but desperately needed.

I've learned that the fastest way to grow is to follow someone who's already walked the path you're on — and then, in turn, become that guide for someone else.

Unshakeable Reminder -

A warrior never walks alone. Seek out those who have gone before you and be willing to guide those who come after.

The path is always clearer when you walk it with a mentor.

"If I have seen further
it is by standing on the shoulders of giants."
- Sir Isaac Newton

Chapter 20 - Service Over Self

"The best way to find yourself
is to lose yourself in the service of others."
- Mahatma Gandhi

Greatness doesn't come from standing above others. It comes from lifting others up.

One of the greatest shifts in my life occurred when I began to live by this principle: Service Over Self. When I stopped asking "What's in it for me?" and started asking "How can I help?", everything changed—my relationships, my business, even my sense of purpose.

In martial arts, we bow before we spar. That bow is more than tradition—it's a moment of humility. It says, "I respect you. I honor your journey. We are here to sharpen one another."

Service is our 'bow' to the world.

I've watched students light up when they're given the chance to mentor others. I've watched leaders transform when they begin focusing on lifting others instead of proving themselves. And I've experienced the healing power of service in my own recovery—when I stopped obsessing about my pain and started walking with others through theirs.

It doesn't take grand gestures. Sometimes, service just shows up. Listening. Encouraging. Making a phone call. Sharing a lesson you've learned the hard way.

Here's the secret: when you give to others, you're also giving to yourself. Not in a transactional way, but in a soul-level way; because we are all wired for connection and contribution.

So keep training. Keep growing. But most of all, keep giving. That's the Black Belt way.

"A true warrior doesn't fight for glory—
he fights for those who can't."
- Brad Wenneberg, Shihan

A True, Unshakeable Warrior

When I think of a warrior, I am reminded of a former student of mine, Brandon Hampson. Even though his life was tragically cut short, he left a lasting legacy which I believe is the definition of a true warrior. Here are my thoughts published in our AMAA June 2005 newsletter.

" 'I would like to introduce you to American Martial Arts Academy's newest and honored Shodan—1st degree Black Belt—20-year-old Mr. Brandon Hampson.'

"These are the words I spoke during a very special Black Belt ceremony on June 22, 2005, in the Hampsons' home. As I and Mrs. Wenneberg and other senior Black Belts gathered around Brandon while he rested on his bed, I couldn't help but reflect on Leadership. You see, Brandon began his journey with AMAA in 1999, and over the time that we have had the honor of sharing his life, he has shown himself to be a true warrior.

"Brandon has always been enthusiastic, full of energy, joy, humor, and an uplifting attitude. He has always been respectful, courteous, generous of spirit, and helping in nature. Although he has had the personal challenge of being hearing-impaired, he never allowed this to negatively influence his efforts or attitude. In class, he always gave 110 percent. He stayed focused and persistent and advanced steadily through the ranks. He assisted the instructors, participated in our specific classes (like weapons), and attended studio activities (like Idyllwild). He always had a 'Black Belt' attitude, and his grace and smile have persisted even through the most horrific of times during the last nine months.

"In September of 2004, Brandon was diagnosed with a brain tumor which has subsequently proved to be a particularly aggressive form of cancer. Since that day, though, Brandon has shown his usual good attitude, humor, and courage in the face of four major brain surgeries, numerous painful procedures and treatments, radiation, chemotherapy, paralysis and seizures. He has amazed all his health care professionals with his zest for life and his good nature and determination.

"As I stood next to Brandon, it was obvious that he had fought a good fight against this horrible disease; and although he is now terminal, the light shines bright in Brandon's eyes and the courage of his spirit can be felt. As I bowed and respectfully handed Brandon his new Black Belt and conferred upon him the rank of Shodan in Goju Shin-Ryu, I knew that the lessons I, and others, had received from Brandon would stay with us forever. Looking into his eyes, pupil to pupil, we both knew that leadership goes both ways and we have learned from each other.

“Leadership is not a gift; you must earn it with your very actions. We lead by how we behave, by our attitude, by our contributions to the world as a whole. We have the opportunity for negative or positive leadership on each and every day. It is in our own hands. Brandon has led through his consistent and unyielding integrity with positive, ethical character, good humor, persistent effort, and undefeatable courage. He has demonstrated what a Black Belt IS by being the best he can be even through the most dreadful of times.

“We are ultimately judged by the way we have lived our life. Brandon’s life is a blessing and a way of courage and leadership. His leadership lives today and forever. I encourage you to learn from his example and to take on the responsibility of leadership no matter the challenges encountered.

- Mr. Hampson passed away on June 26, 2005, at 20 years of age -

“Let’s be people of service—to our parents, our spouse and children, brothers and sisters, friends and co-workers, even strangers. We should lend a helping hand instead of expecting a handout. As I have said before, living life successfully is not for the weak of heart—it is for the strong. When we go to school or work tomorrow, instead of looking for what others can do for us, let’s ask what we can do for them. We should do this expecting nothing in return, and do it every day for the rest of our lives. Going the extra mile today will assure us of success tomorrow.

“A warrior does not have to be physically strong or even possess any special talents. They merely have to be a person who is willing to live for something greater than themself. The battle is between our ears and the eighteen-inch journey from our brains to our hearts. Unless we realize that we can't just think our way into being a warrior and must instead act our way into it, we will never have the connection between head and heart."

"Service to others is the rent you pay for your room here on earth."
- Muhammad Ali

Unshakeable Reminder –

When we shift the focus from me to we, everything changes.

Service isn't sacrifice - it's strength.

Who can we lift today? A small act of kindness might be the spark someone else is waiting for.

Chapter 21 - Show Up Anyway: The Quiet Power of Example

"The true measure of a person is not how they act when things go smoothly - but how they persist when everything hurts."
- adapted from Dr. Martin Luther King, Jr.

I have followed many people's examples over my lifetime. In the early days, I wasn't very selective in my associations. I hung around those who drank like me—partied, hollered, and ran wild until the night's end. Places where I didn't belong. The kind my mom always warned me about it.

I gravitated toward people who were going nowhere—just like I was. Misery and failure were the price of admission. I still remember my mom's warning: *"Hang with the losers, you'll be a loser. Hang with the winners, and you'll be a winner."* Her words turned out to be profoundly true.

I was on a path toward destruction, no ambition, no moral compass. I slipped into alcoholism, not even recognizing what it meant to be a winner. I was completely unarmed for life.

But when I began my recovery and started building a new blueprint for how to live, several things became clear right away. Winners *show up*. They go to work—even when they don't feel like it. They don't make excuses. They take responsibility. They are accountable.

I started to see that this new "culture" was built on timeless principles—values, ethics, and integrity. These weren't just nice ideas. They were action steps.

I wanted what they had—not just success, but peace. Self-respect. I found mentors. I listened. I followed directions. I became honest, open-minded, and willing. And I began to walk the Warrior's path.

My heroes weren't on movie screens or the sports fields. They were the ones who walked the talk. The ones who kept showing up. I'd like to share with you the stories of three such warriors—three men who reminded me, time and time again, what it truly means to be an example.

Chuck G.

Chuck walked into our dojo in 2012—at the ripe age of 82. Braces on both legs, back hunched, he looked like he could barely stand. My first thought was, *"Why are you here? You should be home resting."*

I asked him gently, "What is it you're looking for?"

Chuck straightened up, looked me right in the eye, and said: *"I've always been curious about martial arts. So, I've decided to train."*

That one word—*curious*—was all it took. I wasn't sure how we'd do it, but I told him, "Chuck, I don't know how we'll manage this—but we will."

In those early weeks, we had two Black Belts stand on either side of him to catch him when he lost his balance. He worked on flexibility, balance, strength. He never missed class—not for sniffles, injuries, or frustration.

Even when he physically couldn't train, Chuck showed up with a notepad, transcribed everything I taught (minus the more colorful words!), and emailed us typed-up notes the next day.

Eventually, the braces came off. His balance and strength returned. He wielded his cane with skill and precision. One day, when Tom was picking him up to come to the dojo, Chuck fell face-first on the pavement. Bruised and bloodied, he refused to go home. He showed up, got in line, and trained.

He learned to spar—and he was *good*. At age 89, he was swept during a match and hit hardwood. The class froze in fear; but Chuck popped up, waved us off, and kept sparring.

He earned his Black Belt. Then his 2nd degree. And along the way, he earned something even greater—our admiration and the legacy of being a true martial artist.

Even as he grew frail and the doctors told him to stop, Chuck kept showing up. He no longer trained his body, but he studied martial arts history, took notes, and discovered the spiritual gifts within the arts.

We honored him before he passed, celebrating his life with a montage that left no dry eyes.

When we asked him, "Chuck, after all the pain, why did you keep coming back?"
He smiled and said, *"Because I'm just curious."*
Chuck passed at the age of 92!

Chuck's example lives on in every student. Any time someone complains—headache, sniffles, tired, rough day, excuses—we point to Chuck (we have an honored picture of him on the dojo wall). *"Show up. Be the example."* That's what Black Belt Basics are all about.

Daryl

Daryl came to us in his 40s with a severe neck injury that tilted his head permanently to one side. We weren't sure how to help, but he enrolled anyway. He found brotherhood, confidence, and purpose.

One day during class, I noticed blood dripping from his pant leg. I stopped everything.

"Daryl, roll up your pant leg."

He did—revealing deep gouges and bleeding scrapes on both legs.

"What happened?" I asked.

"I crashed my bike coming down the hill," he replied.

Stunned, I asked, "Why didn't you go to the hospital?"

He looked at me and said, in front of the whole class:
"Because I promised you, I'd be in class tonight."

No further explanation needed. His word was his contract.

"Ninety percent of success is just showing up."
- Woody Allen

Tom B.

Tom's wife Lisa enrolled their son Daniel in 2004. A bit later, Tom joined too, wanting to train alongside his son.

As a retired U.S. Navy officer who served aboard submarines during global conflicts—including 9/11—Tom was disciplined, focused, and humble. While serving as a Naval Reservist, he worked as an engineer and manager at Boeing, where he trained hundreds of engineers.

When he began martial arts training, he was 46 and wanted flexibility and strength. Over time, it also became clear that what he found was community, a return to the camaraderie he missed from the Navy.

Tom and Daniel trained together, but their competitiveness got in the way. I eventually separated them into different classes so they could each focus on their own path. It worked beautifully.

Tom worked long days at Boeing—up at 6 AM, off at 5 PM, then a 45-minute commute home. Yet, he never missed a class. He trained, he assisted, he attended my Business & Instructor course three times, and he never once asked for a paycheck.

He's what we call a '*Warrior: One Who Serves*'.

One day during sparring, Tom took a kick to the upper arm that severed his bicep. Major surgery followed. The doctors told him to quit martial arts permanently.

Let me pause to say: there are times when it's wise to stop training for health reasons. I respect that; but Tom's story is something else.

Within a month of surgery, he showed up at the dojo—with notebook in hand—and said, "I'm ready to train."

He observed. He took notes. He taught seated. He doubled down on his physical therapy. The doctors said he'd never lift his arms high again. Tom disagreed.

Today, he trains with no limitations. No complaints. No drama. Just grit.

He's had shoulder replacement, back pain, hip pain—but he never stops. He tested for his 2nd degree Black Belt *sitting in a chair*, modifying techniques and passing with flying colors.

His example teaches us that the only thing that truly limits us... is us.

His son Daniel, who also earned his Black Belt, became a decorated soldier in the United States Army and now serves as a police officer. Their daughter, though she never trained, grew up around the dojo and is now a successful adult.

Lisa remains a dedicated supporter of the martial arts, engaging and volunteering in various other community activities, and being a key leader for the after-school and camp programs at the dojo.

We are blessed to know them. Their story is part of our story.

Unshakeable Reminder -

There are many reasons not to show up; but it only takes *one reason that matters* to stay the course.

Be an example, especially when it's hard. That's how legacy is built.

"You don't have to be perfect, just present."
- Author Unknown

Chapter 22 - Noise-Canceling Headphones

"Don't believe everything you think."
- Allan Lokos

This might seem like a strange topic for a chapter but stay with me—because this one's personal.

If you're anything like me, you've probably heard voices in your head. Not the kind that need medication, the kind that whisper lies.

You're different.

You're weird.

You're not enough.

You're stupid.

You're a failure.

Where did these voices come from? For me, they started with words spoken to me as a child—words that burrowed in and became beliefs. My mom, for reasons I've tried to understand, often tore me down instead of building me up. Over time, those voices became my inner soundtrack.

Eventually, I could identify four distinct voices:

1. The Kid – playful, carefree, full of life.
2. The Teen – rebellious, confused, and convinced he knew everything.

3. The Adult – mature, responsible, capable of reason and sound judgment.
4. The Judge – harsh, punitive, and often wrong.

It was the Judge who did the most damage. He drowned out the others and made me believe I was doomed to self-destruct.

To cope, I turned to alcohol and drugs. At first, they silenced the voices. That was the trap. Eventually, they became the loudest voice in the room—until I couldn't hear anything else.

Recovery saved my life, but it didn't happen all at once. First came the physical healing—abstinence. Then, slowly, came emotional and spiritual healing. I began to feel again... and that wasn't easy. Pain came back. Insecurity. Doubt. But this time, I had tools—principles, rituals, and disciplines I had built in recovery and martial arts. My blueprint for living.

When I drifted from the basics—stopped doing what got me well—the voices crept back in. The Judge cleared his throat, ready to resume his post.

One day, I bought a pair of noise-canceling headphones. I unpacked them, charged them, and put them on. As soon as I flipped the switch, everything went quiet. No hum of appliances, no barking dogs, no ambient chaos—just silence.

That's when it hit me.

It was never the outside noise that was the real problem. It was the noise inside my own head.

With nothing else to drown them out, the voices were loud and clear. I realized that if I didn't stay grounded in my truth, if I didn't stay connected to my spiritual and mental practices, those voices would always be waiting to take over.

I needed to return to the fundamentals—just like a martial artist who forgets his stance and loses his power. The tools in my blueprint still worked: daily routines, positive self-talk, service, prayer, and discipline. The voices were still there, but now I was equipped to keep them in check.

One day, a mentor friend of mine called and said, "Be at my house at 9 AM tomorrow. We are going to the beach."

I was excited. I showed up early, beach-ready, only to find him in his pajamas and robe.

"You're ready," he said, "but I'm not coming with you."

I was stunned.

He looked at me and said, "Brad, you're going to the beach with your best friend—yourself. Get to know him. He's smart, funny, talented, and strong. He's enough. Spend the day with the man I know you are."

It felt like a gut punch—but he was right.

There's an old African proverb that says:

"When there is no enemy within, the enemies outside cannot hurt you."

The problem was never the external voices. The problem was the ones I allowed to live rent-free in my head. And the solution wasn't more noise—it was self-respect, awareness, and practice.

These days, I still have to check in with myself. I still wear metaphorical headphones; but now I don't use them to block the world out—I use them to tune in to the truth:

That I am loved.

That I am worthy.

That I have purpose.

And so do you.

"The loudest voice isn't always the truest.
Learn to listen beyond the noise."
- Brad Wenneberg, Shihan

Unshakeable Reminder -

The loudest battles we fight are often inside our own minds.

Let's ask ourselves: Are we listening to truth—or to lies that don't belong to us anymore?

Turn down the inner noise. Turn up awareness.

Live from the truth that sets you free.

Chapter 23 - Between the Bows - A Warrior's Day

"Rituals are the bows we take to remind ourselves we're still becoming."
- Brad Wenneberg, Shihan

The Opening Bow

We begin.
We live.
We reflect.
We rest.

What we do between those two sacred bookends — that space between the bow in and the bow out — is what defines us.
It reveals our training, our truth, and our trajectory.

This chapter isn't about the final bow - that comes later.
This is about the everyday bow — the daily rituals, the mindful moments, the silent commitments we make to live on purpose.

Long before we take our final stance, we get the chance to bow into the day, and to do it with meaning.

I haven't always been great in the mornings. Some days I didn't want to rise at all. Anger, fear, and the grip of old voices nearly kept me down; but over time, I built a system — a rhythm — that helps me begin each day like a warrior.

It's not perfect, but it's intentional.

The Types of Bows

Each bow we take in the dojo carries weight. Not just physical - also spiritual - and every one of them has a mirror in real life. Let's explore them — and I'll walk you through my day between the bows.

All these physical bows are real — and powerful. But the deeper training? That happens outside the dojo. In the car. At the kitchen table. During hard conversations and quiet choices.

Let me show you how I work to bow throughout my day — not just with my head, but with my heart.

1. Bowing as You Enter the Dojo

"A breath and letting go of the outside stuff, preparing for a great workout."

Life application:
Every threshold is an invitation to release and refocus.
When I enter my home, my office, or a conversation — I mentally "bow in."
I try to leave behind the chaos and enter with presence.

2. Bowing Onto the Mat

"A sacred bow — stepping into a place filled with history, legacy, sweat, blood, and tears."

Life application:
Stepping into responsibility, leadership, or parenting deserves that same reverence.
We honor the work that came before us, and the sacred space we

now occupy.
It's not just a mat. It's a mission field.

3. Bowing to the Front

"A serious, introspective moment to center yourself — ready to perform, focus, demand more of yourself, and show deep respect."

Life application:
Before a meeting, a performance, or even a tough decision — I pause. I center.
This is where I check my ego, reset my attitude, and ask:
Am I showing up with excellence, or just showing up?

4. Bowing to Each Other

"Mutual respect, honor, camaraderie, friendship. Acknowledging the shared journey."

Life application:
This is in every handshake. Every "I see you." Every act of kindness.
Whether it's family, student, or stranger — I try to bow with my actions, not just my head.
Respect isn't a concept. It's a commitment.

5. Bowing Off the Mat

"A moment of gratitude - honoring the training and the lessons just learned."

Life application:
At the end of a task, a conversation, or a challenge — I ask: What did I learn?

Gratitude reframes struggle. If I can bow out thankful, then I never walk away empty.

6. Bowing Out of the Studio

"A symbolic preparation for life's next adventure — leaving with your spiritual battery recharged."

Life application:

Every transition deserves a bow.
When I leave the dojo, I remind myself: I've been filled so I can go fill others.
Recharge. Then serve.

7. Metaphorical Bows Throughout the Day

"We bow through the day — moments of pause, respect, intention, and renewal in everyday life."

Life application:

A deep breath before speaking.
A pause before reacting.
A whisper of gratitude before sleep.
These are the quiet bows of a mindful life.

I want to share with you about my day -
Not because it's perfect - but because it's intentional.

I didn't always understand the importance of these rituals. In fact for years, I stumbled through the day on autopilot; but life has taught me that we become what we repeatedly do. So now, I live my day between the bows.

1. Morning Meditation

This is where I hit the spiritual “reset” button.
Sometimes it’s silent. Sometimes it’s spoken.
Usually, it’s simple:
“God, guide my words, my actions, and my heart today.”

Some days, I pray before my feet hit the ground.
Some days, I grumble a bit first.
But either way, I bow inward before I face the outward.

2. A Thought for the Day

This thought could come from an AA daily reader, a devotional, or a note I’ve written to myself.
If it says “progress, not perfection,” I loosen the grip of shame.
If it says, “pause when agitated,” I pause... eventually.
The goal isn’t perfection. It’s alignment.

3. Positive Input Only

I don’t let morning news or raging talk radio hijack my mindset.
Instead, I put on happy music - usually something from the 50s - my favorites: Elvis. Frankie Valli. Sometimes a little doo-wop or Hawaiian guitar.

Fun fact: my drive home from the studio is 15 minutes.
My favorite Hawaiian track is 4.5 minutes long.
I play it three times, and the last strum hits just about as I hit my driveway.

Intentional.

4. Affirmations

I surround myself — literally — with truth.
- "You are a man of purpose."
- "You are sober. You are strong. You are free."
- "Integrity is your compass. Love is your guide."

These aren't motivational slogans.
They are anchors, especially for when the wind picks up.

5. Protecting My Mindset

I don't engage in gossip or negative talk - I guard against that in my day.
If someone's 'off energy' enters my space, I can offer grace... and I don't have to absorb it.
The bow here? It's a bow to boundaries.

6. Surrounding Myself with Winners

The company we keep has a powerful influence on our behavior and mindset.
I keep close to people who are moving forward.

Not flawless — but focused.
Not loud — but living with integrity.

"If you run with the wounded,
don't be surprised when you start limping."
- Brad Wenneberg, Shihan

Now, I walk with warriors. I bow to those becoming, not just those performing.

These aren't just habits. They're rituals. And rituals are sacred — because they shape the man I bring into every room, every dojo, every conversation, every relationship.

A Quiet Bow, A Fierce Goodbye

She came in the back door of the dojo.
Head down. Shoulders slumped. Eyes cast low.
Her name was Linda.
She said she wanted to try a class "just to get some confidence."
But we knew there was more. Her silence spoke volumes.

Her *gi* didn't fit her body or her spirit.
She drifted during partner work, hoping not to be seen.
But we saw her — not to call her out, but to call her in.

Over time, her *kiai* grew from a whisper to a roar.
Her back straightened. Her voice steadied. Her presence expanded.

Eventually, she left the man who tried to erase her.
She didn't announce it.
She bowed.

That bow wasn't about submission.
It was a battle cry of reclaiming.

Today, Linda helps new students tie their belts.
She laughs easily. She bows with pride.
Every time she enters and exits the mat, I see it.
That isn't just a routine. It's a reminder.
She's still standing.
Like a warrior does.

Unshakeable Reminder -

Where in your day could you pause and bow?
To someone you've overlooked.
To a moment you've rushed past.
To the truth of who you're becoming.

We don't just bow in the dojo.
We bow in traffic. In tension. In triumph. In joys.

Bowing is not a weakness. It's Warrior wisdom.
So today, between your first breath and your final yawn...
Bow with intention.

One day, I'll take my final bow... but today isn't that day.
Today, I bowed by how I showed up between the bells, between the tasks, between the chaos.
Between the bows, I am becoming.

"The warrior doesn't just train for the battle — he trains for the moments in between. That's where character is forged. That's where legacy is built."
- Brad Wenneberg, Shihan

Chapter 24 - Personal Freedom

"Freedom is not the absence of commitments, but the ability to choose—and commit myself to—what is best for me."
- Paulo Coelho

I was born in the United States of America—a free country. From as far back as I can remember, I was told—not always by my parents, but by society in general—that I was free to be whatever I dreamed of being. This is the land of opportunity. We can travel at will, eat what and where we please, choose our work, go to school, and vote on matters of local and national importance. The freedoms we enjoy in America are almost too numerous to count. And yet...

In this chapter, I want to share what personal freedom means to me; because even in a free society, many of us live in prisons of our own making—trapped by fear, ego, addiction, resentment, and apathy. We become slaves to our own comfort zones and forget to cherish the very opportunities that freedom provides.

Freedom is not free. It must be earned—especially personal freedom. It's not handed to us on a silver platter. That's why so many immigrants come to this country, seize the opportunities, and rise to success. They appreciate freedom. They recognize it as an opportunity, not a gift.

In 1991, my life looked solid. I was 38 years old, married, a father of two, a homeowner with money in the bank, and eight years sober. I went to four AA meetings a week, working closely with my mentor, and helping others. Life was good.

But pride crept in.
I started skipping meetings. I stopped calling my sponsor. I stopped serving others. I took all the credit. I believed I was in control.

So, one day, I walked out the front door, straight to the liquor store, bought a bottle of vodka, and toasted to my "freedom." That toast nearly killed me. I stayed drunk until I hit an all-time low. When my mentor found me, I was nearly dead—so close, in fact, that the ER staff called for a rabbi to administer last rites.

That bottom almost cost me everything—my wife, my children, my career, my dignity, and my life.

That's when I truly learned: Personal freedom is not about doing what I want. It's about choosing what is right. And it's something I must earn—every day, every moment.

As a young man, I lived as a prisoner of self: selfish, afraid, insecure, angry, and full of blame. I drank to escape, to numb, to cope. True freedom only came when I was willing to face myself and fight for something better.

"You can be in prison and still be free.
You can be free and still be in prison."
- Victor Frankl

I had to start by admitting the truth: I was lazy, selfish, self-centered, and full of fear. I was an alcoholic. I was powerless over people, places, and things. The only thing I had any control over was my actions, my attitude, my choices.

No one else was responsible for my behavior; and although I didn't have an ideal childhood, it was my job to do the repairs. That's when I became a peaceful warrior.

Once I accepted those truths, I had a choice: keep living in chains or stepping over the line and fight for my freedom. That's when the IDEA Factor kicked in:

Identify the problen,
Decide to change,
Enthusiasm for the solution,
Action toward growth.

I entered recovery. I studied business. I found new mentors. I became teachable.
I learned how to love, how to serve, how to grow up and show up. And as I took ownership of my own inner life, the outer chains fell away.

My fear was replaced with faith. My relationships began to heal. My confidence grew. My selfishness turned to service. I gave more than I expected to receive—and in return, God gave me back my life.

I stopped 'just believing' that freedom was possible—and I started knowing it.

"None are more hopelessly enslaved, than those who falsely believe they are free."
- Johann Wolfgang von Goethe

Many of us are agnostic—not just spiritually, but in life. We hesitate to commit. We don't know until we've experienced something for ourselves. I believed I loved Bonnie in 1970. After over 50 years of marriage, I know I love her.

I believed I could become a police officer. When I was sworn in, I knew I had made it.

I believed I could get sober. When I stayed sober, I knew it was possible.

I believed I could be free. And now, I know it.

As a martial artist and teacher, it's my duty and my privilege to help others move from bondage to freedom—body, mind, and spirit. I've watched students move from self-doubt to self-respect, from fear to courage, from believing to knowing.

One of the tools that helped me most on that journey was this:

The Serenity Prayer

God, grant me the serenity to accept the things I cannot change,
Courage to change the things I can,
And the wisdom to know the difference.

I say it daily. Sometimes hourly. Especially when I start trying to control people, places, and things. My serenity is directly linked to how much I accept what I cannot control—and how courageous I am in facing what I can.

"Everything can be taken from a man but one thing: the last of the human freedoms - to choose one's attitude in any given set of circumstances."
- Viktor Frankl

The Elephant and the Rope

There's a story about a man who visited a traveling circus. Behind the tents, he noticed something strange—massive elephants standing calmly, tied to tiny stakes in the ground with thin ropes.

No chains. No cages. Just a simple rope.

He asked a trainer, "Why don't the elephants break free?"

The trainer replied,
"When they're babies, the rope is strong enough to hold them. They pull and struggle, but they can't break free. Eventually, they stop trying. And when they grow up, they still believe they can't escape. So, they don't."

These mighty elephants remain bound—not by the rope—but by the **lie they believe**.

So do we.

Many of us stay stuck because of a belief we adopted years ago:
I can't.
I'm not good enough.
This is just who I am.

But we're not that child anymore. The rope no longer has power—unless we hand it back.

It's time to pull up the stake.
Test the lie.
Walk free.

Unshakeable Reminder -

Freedom isn't just a flag or a vote. It's a choice we make in how we live. Don't wait to be rescued. Choose to break free from whatever binds you—fear, ego, doubt, or addiction. The key is already in your hand.

"Discipline is the bridge between who we are
and who we could be.
And on that bridge, freedom walks."
- adapted from Jim Rohn

Chapter 25 - It's the Experience... Not the Roller Coaster

- Designing Moments that People Can't Wait to Come Back To -

People often ask what our "secret sauce" is at the karate school — how we've managed to build something special not just in business, but at home and in life. Most assume it must be *karate*. They say, "Your techniques must be so good that people just keep coming back."

That's not it.

We're not in the karate business — we're in the **experience** business.

Yes, people come to our school for martial arts. But they *stay* because of the way they **feel** when they're here. That same "Unshakeable" magic is what transforms marriages, families, and spiritual lives too — **not what we do, but the experience we create.**

Think about it: every day we are flooded with negative experiences.
Headlines. Honking horns. Arguments. Deadlines. The word "No." Store clerks with no smile, bosses with no mercy, kids who won't listen... it wears on us.

Now picture a family of four walking into Disneyland. Mom and Dad are already stressed — *$500 just to get in the gate?* They're thinking, *this better be worth it.*

And then something happens...

Music. Bright colors. Big smiles. Balloon vendors. Mickey and Minnie twirling in the streets. Suddenly the real world falls away. No boss. No chores. No arguing. Just pure **experience**. At the end of the night — muscles aching, wallets empty, kids wired — what do they say?
"That was amazing. I can't wait to come back."

Not because the roller coaster was technically superior — but because the **experience** made them *feel alive*.

Creating the Magic, the Experience

That's exactly what we strive to create at American Martial Arts Academy. Tuition, uniforms, time — it looks like a big investment. But the moment they walk through our doors, everything feels different:

- Someone smiles and greets them by name.
- The energy is bright and alive.
- They are encouraged, believed in, and lifted up.

You will never hear these words here:
No. You're wrong. Stop doing that. What's wrong with you? Bad.
(Children, teens, and adults hear that all day in the real world — they don't need to pay us to feel worse.)

Parents return week after week not just because their child is learning kick-punch-block... but because the family is experiencing JOY, SAFETY, COMMUNITY, and GROWTH. The karate is just the roller coaster.

Now here's the real takeaway: you and I can create this same kind of **"experience" at home**.

- Turn off the news when your spouse walks in — greet them like you haven't seen them in a month.
- Light a candle in the kitchen and turn dinner into a *date*, not a duty.
- Slip a kind and encouraging note into your child's backpack.
- Leave early for traffic and sing your favorite songs.
- Choose to become the person who **creates moments worth coming back to**.

Why come home to the same old routine every day when you can *design experiences* that your loved ones never want to leave?

That is the true secret to success — in business, marriage, family, friendship, and faith — creating an *Unshakeable* experience of love, joy, encouragement, and presence wherever you go.

Unshakeable Reminder -

"Design experiences that people never want to leave — and they'll stay loyal for life."
- Brad Wenneberg, Shihan

Chapter 26 - The Value of Humor

- Confessions from the Dojo -

"Life is too important to be taken seriously."
- Oscar Wilde

If you can laugh, you can last.
Humor is one of the most underrated strengths of a warrior. In our dojo, we teach seriousness with a smile. Life is hard enough - why not lighten the load with laughter?

Some of my most powerful teaching moments came not during deep lectures, but through jokes that slipped truth in through the back door.

Humor keeps us humble. It reminds us not to take ourselves too seriously. It's the release valve for pressure, stress, and ego.

I've had to laugh at myself countless times—whether fumbling through a kata or forgetting my own advice. Humor gives us grace.

In recovery, humor helped me survive the dark nights. In marriage, it helped Bonnie and I bridge the tough moments. In business, it helped me bounce back from big mistakes.

Laughter builds connection. It disarms tension. It opens people up. Even in the middle of a sparring match or a serious belt exam, a well-timed chuckle can shift the tense energy and reset the spirit.

So yes—be serious about your growth. But don't be so serious that you forget to smile.

Let your journey be strong... but let it also be joyful.

"A good laugh heals a lot of hurts."
- Madeleine L'Engle

Smokin' Shoes and the Campfire Shuffle

It was a chilly evening at our annual mountain retreat in Black Mountain, Riverside County, California. I started this retreat in 1994 to connect with students and their families beyond the dojo. It quickly became a favorite tradition—twenty-five years of laughter, learning, and occasional misadventure.

This particular night, it was just CJ and I around the campfire. Late. Quiet. Cold. We were both relaxed, enjoying the warmth and the silence. Eventually, we dozed off in our chairs, lulled by the crackle of the fire and the peace of the mountains.

What happened next still makes me laugh to this day.

I woke up first—probably only five minutes had passed—but something smelled off. I glanced down and saw smoke. CJ's tennis shoes were starting to smolder. Within moments, the soles began to melt.

Right then, CJ woke up with a loud scream. Startled and "hot-footed," he leapt up and started dancing around the campsite like his life depended on it—yelling, "I'm on fire! I'm on fire!" and stomping wildly in the dirt.

Once he finally cooled down, he looked at me—wide-eyed—and asked, "Why didn't you tell me?!"

I replied, truthfully, "I just woke up in time to witness the carnage of your frantic dance of pain."

We laughed. Hard. His feet were fine... his shoes, not so much.

He got a new pair. I got a story I've been telling ever since.

Unshakeable Reminder –

Sometimes we sleep a little too close to the fire. That's life. What matters is how we respond when things heat up. Laugh when you can, learn what you need, and always keep an extra pair of shoes handy—just in case.

The Triple Threat

It started like any normal day at the dojo: three floors humming with energy, kids in crisp uniforms, instructors in rhythm, parents sipping coffee. We were firing on all cylinders.

Until... it all hit the fan. Literally.

First class of the day: one of our youngest students had a wardrobe malfunction of the urinary variety—right in the middle of the mat. His little gi pants hit the floor like a white flag of surrender. No big deal. We've seen worse. We cleaned it up, sanitized the mat, gave high-fives all around, and pressed on.

Second class: as soon as we bowed in, another young student froze mid-kata. There was a look of distress, and then... the dreaded "code brown." Higher stakes. Messier cleanup. More air freshener.

Third class: a big dog bolted in—no leash, no owner, just pure chaos. He galloped across the mat like he was going for his black belt, lifted a leg, and—yes—marked his territory with the confidence of a Shih Tzu on a mission.

We had to shut down the dojo for two full days to clean, fumigate, and spiritually sage the place.

Unshakeable Reminder -

The dojo is not just a place of discipline—it's a stage for divine comedy.

Pepper Spray Curiosity - aka: the Day the Dojo Needed a Biohazard Suit

Never miss an opportunity to laugh—and laugh out loud with gusto. Humor is especially impactful when we learn to laugh at ourselves. What you're about to read is 100% true. No dojos were permanently harmed in the making of this memory.

I was sitting in my office one afternoon and noticed a bottle of pepper spray on the desk. I wondered, *Is this expired?*

Naturally, I tested it. Indoors.

Ten minutes later, my eyes were burning, students and staff were coughing, and our Program Director fled the building with new prospective students trailing behind in full-blown chemical warfare retreat.

We had to evacuate the dojo again and cancel classes. For two days, we ran fans and flushed the place out.

My pepper spray privileges were permanently revoked.

"If you can't laugh at yourself ... don't worry,
your students will do it for you."
- Brad Wenneberg, Shihan

Knocked Down and Called Out

Decades ago, my Sensei and a handful of students traveled to a karate tournament. I had competed dozens of times before and was quite good—especially in sparring.

We trained hard, and I was ready.

I competed in *kata* first... and won! I was flying high. Confidence turned quickly to ego.

Then came my sparring match. My opponent? A younger female competitor. I had more experience and, I'll admit, thought she was cute.

We bowed in... and I made a crucial, painful mistake.

I winked at her.

"Fight!" the sparring commander shouted.

Next thing I knew, I was flat on my back.

She had spun a perfect crescent kick right to my head. Lights blurry. Crowd quiet. Pride bruised.

She calmly looked down at me and said, "Never wink at me again."

Ouch.

My Sensei ran over and demanded, “What the hell happened?”

I told him.

He shook his head and said, “Get your ego in check, or that won’t be your only knock-down today.”

I finished the tournament with two black eyes… and one big lesson in humility.

Spider Sense… Zero

We were once again moving into a larger facility to accommodate our rapidly growing student body. During the build-out, three of my high-ranking Black Belts were assigned to paint a massive 14-foot wall.

Earlier that day, our front office staff member—equal parts administrator, ninja, and prankster—planted a giant fake spider high up where the ‘painters’ would spot it.

When they saw it, chaos broke out.

“You get it!”

“No way—you get it!”

They hurled shoes, paintbrushes, even a water bottle at it. One brave soul climbed halfway up the ladder and took a swing—missed.

Again and again, they launched aerial attacks, shouting and squealing like kids in a haunted house.

Finally, our fearless front desk warrior calmly climbed the ladder, plucked the fake spider off the wall, and tossed it at the shrieking Black Belts below.

The roar of her laughter nearly knocked her off the ladder.

The dojo may build champions—but nobody is safe from a good prank.

Superman and Rule 62 (Jack C.)

There was a man in one of my early AA meetings named **Jack C.**

I loved this man. He was sharp, funny, and always had something to say about ego.

"Drop the ego," he'd grin. "You're not a big shot."

One day I noticed he wore a shiny medallion—bright red and gold, with a big Superman "S."

"Seriously?" I asked. "You preach humility, and you're wearing Superman's logo?"

Jack laughed. "Come here, son."

He turned the medallion around.

On the back were two simple words: **Rule 62**.

"Look it up," he said with a wink.

I did.

Rule 62: Don't take yourself too damn seriously.

Jack wore the 'S' not to show off—but to remind himself (and the rest of us) that even Superman needs a sense of humor.

That lesson has stayed with me ever since.

Unshakeable Reminder –

Laughter is medicine - and a marker of perspective. When we can laugh at ourselves, we loosen the grip of fear and ego. Let's make room for joy, even in the serious work. Humor keeps us human - and keeps the dojo - and our lives - light.

The dojo teaches us more than strikes and stances. It teaches us to fall, to laugh, to get up, and bow anyway.

Next time life knocks you down - or you get too close to the fire, you get knocked out, fumigate your own office, or outwitted by a fake spider - remember:

<u>Rule 62: Don't take yourself too seriously</u>.
Laugh, learn, and live to bow again.

Chapter 27 - Soar Like an Eagle

(*Unshakeable* Edition)

"I choose to soar like an eagle—wise and strong—
above the storm, directed toward purpose, joy, and freedom.
I refuse to give in or stop climbing.
I am a warrior."
- Brad Wenneberg, Shihan

Did you know that an eagle can sense when a storm is coming—long before the skies grow dark? When the wind begins to stir, the eagle flies to a high place, locks its wings, and waits. And when the storm hits, it doesn't flee.

It rises.

The same wind that threatens destruction becomes its lift.

That image stuck with me the first time I heard it. I saw myself in that eagle—not because I was soaring, but because I was stuck in the storm, flapping against the wind, worn out and grounded by life. What I didn't know then is what I've learned through recovery, martial arts, and faith:

You don't have to escape the storm.
You learn to ride it.

Every one of us will face turbulence, sickness, setbacks, failure, loss. The question is: Will it bury us or build us?
Will we get bitter or get better?

When we rely on something greater than ourselves—what I call God—and anchor into truth, we discover a strength we didn't know we had. That's not theory. That's survival. That's what changed me from a man running from the storm, to one who now teaches others how to rise through it.

If I'm honest, I've lived two very different lives. The first was a mess of ego, addiction, dishonesty, and selfishness. I was a taker. I stole peace from others and robbed myself of purpose. The second life began the day I stopped blaming and started taking responsibility. I got sober. I surrendered. I suited up. I stepped onto the mat and began to walk the Warrior's Way.

The difference between those two lives wasn't luck.
It was choice.

We don't soar by chance—we soar by intention.

I've chosen to live by a code—one rooted in honor, humility, integrity, and service. I'm not perfect. But I'm free. Not because life is easy, but because I've stopped running from it.

If you're reading this and feel grounded by fear, shame, or failure, know this: eagles are meant to fly, and warriors are made in the wind.

It's not about what you've done. It's about what you're doing now. We all have moments where we forget who we are. The key is to remember we are not victims. We are not our past. We are not broken beyond repair.

We are worth the effort.
We have something to give.
And we were born to rise.

No one can steal your dream unless you hand it over. So stop waiting for permission. Stop giving in to doom and gloom. Don't let the critics, the naysayers, or your own negative self-talk dictate your flight path.

Bamboo and the Samurai

There's an old story of a samurai who stood before a mighty storm. He watched as trees were bent and broken, limbs cracking under pressure.

Except for one: a grove of bamboo, bending low but never breaking.

After the storm passed, the samurai approached a monk and asked, "Why does the bamboo endure, while the oak shatters?"

The monk replied, "Because the bamboo does not resist the wind—it bows to it. Then, when the storm passes, it rises again. Strength is not in defiance. It is in flexibility."

That story became one of the great lessons in my life.

I used to try to muscle through everything—resisting pain, pushing people away, pretending I didn't need help. But it wasn't until I bent, until I surrendered, that I began to rise with grace and power. Despite storms that still come, I've been able to bend to become unshakeable.

The storm is not your enemy.
It's your teacher.
Soar like an eagle.
Bend like bamboo.
Become unshakeable in spite of life's challenges.
That's the way of the Warrior.

Unshakeable Reminder -

Storms will come. But they are not your enemy.
They are your proving ground.
Lock your wings, trust your strength, and rise.
The view is truly better from up here.

Chapter 28 - A Warrior's Way Through Change

"I thought I needed to be who I was.
Life showed me I needed to become who I could be."
- Hanya Yanagihara

The Fear of Change

For a long time, the word *change* made me flinch.

I'd hear it and think: *Oh no, not again. I can't handle more change.* My self-talk would spiral: *What if I'm not ready? What if I lose what I've built?*
What if I'm not enough in the next season?

It was as if every new door came with a warning sign:

DANGER—UNFAMILIAR TERRITORY AHEAD.

The irony is that 'change' is the only thing in life that's guaranteed. It's also the very thing that can make life beautiful—if we stop fighting it and start walking through it.

It took me years to learn that.
It took pain, aging, loss, surgery, letting go, and surrender.
But what I've discovered is simple and unshakeable:

Fear makes change feel like a curse.
Faith reveals it as a gift.

A Warrior's Shift: Second Chances and a Haircut

After my cancer surgery, I found myself in a place I hadn't visited in years: deep discouragement.

Six months into recovery, I was feeling frustrated and defeated. I couldn't do what I used to. My body felt foreign. My energy was different. I was still here—but I didn't feel *alive*.

Then one day I went in for a simple haircut.

My stylist looked at me kindly and said,

"It must feel like a blessing... getting a second chance."

I didn't have a comeback. I just sat there.

Because I realized—I had missed the point.

I was so caught up in mourning the man I used to be that I hadn't made space for the man I was becoming.
I had survived something big. I had another shot. And I was wasting it with self-pity.

That day marked a turning point.

I stopped asking *"Why me?"* and started asking *"What now?"*

I started counting my blessings again—daily.
I began working hard not just at recovery, but at **letting go of what I used to be and honoring what I still could be.**

Intimacy had to look different. Strength had to look different. But love? Gratitude? Courage? Those things never needed fixing.

Change didn't steal my purpose, it refined it.

When the Mat Changes Beneath You

I'm 72 now.

That number carries a lot - decades of teaching, thousands of students, a dojo full of memories - but it also brings change.

These days, I can't perform on the mat like I once did.
I use a stool now during certain classes because standing for long stretches is tough. My body, a once-dependable machine, now whispers (and sometimes shouts), *"Slow down."*

My role at the academy has changed. I'm not the day-to-day operations guy anymore. The younger generation, my children, our instructors—have stepped up and lead with strength and vision. And I couldn't be prouder.

But, I'd be lying if I said it was easy to step back.

There's a grief that comes with aging—not just of ability, but of identity.
I had to confront the question: *Who am I if I'm not "Shihan on the mat" every day?*

And the answer came quietly:

I am still a warrior—but my sword now is wisdom, not speed.

I've learned that legacy isn't in how many punches you throw...
It's in the long-lasting impact and influence that you've had on others and future generations.
It's in how many leaders you raise.

The Turn Left Principle

Years ago, I had a habit: whenever I wanted something in life, I'd charge at it headfirst—no matter what stood in my way.

And when I hit a wall? I'd back up... and charge again. Over and over. Until I was bloodied, bruised, and no closer to the goal.

A wise mentor once said to me,

"If you hit the wall... turn left."

That advice changed my life.

Sometimes the wall is the sign.
Sometimes the thing we want isn't what we *need.*
And sometimes the path forward means surrendering the plan we wrote in our head and stepping into the purpose waiting at our side.

When I finally "turned left" in my marriage, stopped demanding, and started serving Bonnie's needs—our entire relationship changed.
When I turned left after cancer surgery, I stopped grieving my past and started embracing my future.
When I turned left in leadership, I stepped aside to lift up the next generation—and in doing so, honored the art I love.

Changing for Love

Of all the walls I've hit, the one in my marriage was the thickest.

Bonnie and I struggled for decades over the same issue. She longed for affection and emotional connection. I wanted physical intimacy. I kept insisting, "I'm just not the affectionate type." That was my story, and I clung to it like a black belt that hadn't been earned.

We tried counseling. We talked. We argued. And we kept hitting the wall.

Then one afternoon in 2000, exhausted and frustrated, I went home and took a nap. Before I closed my eyes, I said a prayer: "God, I'm willing to turn left."

When I woke up, something had shifted. For years, I'd been trying to change my wife—to meet my needs. But love doesn't demand change from others. It demands transformation from within.

I started giving Bonnie the affection she deserved—not because it was easy, but because it brought her joy. And when I began fulfilling her needs, mine were met tenfold. The wall vanished.

That's Black Belt love: service over self, even when it's uncomfortable.

"A Black Belt is simply a white belt who was willing to change, again and again."
- Martial Arts Wisdom

The Blessing of Change

Change stripped me.
Then it softened me.
Then it blessed me.

It taught me that my value doesn't come from what I *do*—but from how I *love,* how I *serve*, and how I *lead with humility.*

Yes, I'm still dealing with physical pain.
Yes, I'm still learning to accept what I cannot do.
But I'm also celebrating what I *can* do:

- Mentor future Black Belts
- Write the lessons I've lived
- Show up with grace and wisdom
- And whisper to myself and others, when needed, *"Turn left."*

Change is not the enemy. It's the Sensei we never asked for—firm but faithful.

If we're willing to listen, it will teach us what youth never could:

That strength isn't in what we hold on to. It's in what we're willing to release.

Unshakeable Reminder -

Change isn't the end of the path—it's the next bow on your journey. Bow with honor. Walk with faith. Turn left when needed.

"Change is the belt we never take off.
The warrior doesn't chase comfort—he chases growth."
- Brad Wenneberg, Shihan

Chapter 29 - The Flinch

"We can't train the flinch out of us.
But we can train how we respond to it."
- Tony Blauer

The Crack of the Bat

In martial arts, we learn to accept one simple truth:
The flinch is unavoidable.

It doesn't matter how long you've trained, how high your rank, or how calm your spirit—the flinch is part of being human.

Now imagine this...

You're at a baseball game on a warm summer day. A crack of the bat rings out, and suddenly a ball is flying straight toward your face at 100 miles an hour.

Instinctively—before your brain even registers what's happening, your hands shoot up to protect yourself. That's the flinch.

But here's the difference...

Someone without training may freeze, shield the wrong way, and get hit square in the face.

But someone trained in Black Belt Basics?

They flinch, yes—but then they rotate their body. They angle just enough to deflect the impact. Maybe they even catch the ball. Maybe they walk away with a souvenir instead of a broken nose.

The flinch still happens.
But the *response* changes everything.

The Flinch in Life

In life, the flinch shows up in more subtle—and more damaging—ways.

Not just physically; but also Emotionally, Spiritually, Relationally.

When I was a boy—around eight or nine years old—I was physically and emotionally abused by a close family member. I don't blame him anymore. I've come to understand that he was likely repeating what was done to him.

But still... it left marks.

Scars that didn't always show up in bruises, but in reflexes - physical AND emotional reflexes.

As a grown man, whenever someone touched me unexpectedly—even in affection—I would flinch. I'd pull away. Bonnie, my wife, didn't understand at first. She thought maybe she had done something wrong.

But it wasn't her hand I was reacting to.
It was **my past**.

The 9-year-old inside me still lived in my nervous system.
And that child was still flinching.

When we came to understand that together, Bonnie stopped taking it personally. And I went to work—on healing, on awareness, on training the deeper response.

Emotional Reflexes Are Still Reflexes

Here's another example.

My mother was strong, loud, and intense. If I came home with the wrong kind of milk, she'd yell, call me stupid, shame me. It was routine. I grew up flinching at feedback.

Years later, I'm a grown man—married, respected, successful.

And I brought home the wrong thing from the store.

Bonnie, kindly, said, *"Oh, I think you grabbed the wrong kind."*

No anger. No judgment. Just a comment.

And yet—**the flinch**.

Not in my hands. In my soul.

My nervous system wasn't hearing my wife's voice.
It was hearing my mother's.

That's how deeply these flinches live in us.
We think we've outgrown them; but they're hiding in our reactions, our defensiveness, our distance.

So, What Do We Do? How Do We Become Unshakeable?

We train.

Not to remove the flinch...
But to *understand* it.
To *honor* where it came from.
To *respond* with awareness, not reflex.

Just like in martial arts, we don't expect our students to stop flinching overnight. We train them to breathe, to move, to block, to rotate, to recover.

Same in life.

"Everyone flinches. The difference is what happens next."
- Julien Smith

Here's the process I've learned:

- **Recognition** – I notice the flinch. I admit it's there. I stop pretending.
- **Acceptance** – I stop judging it. It's part of my story. I honor the boy behind it.
- **Mentorship** – Sometimes I need help. From a sponsor. A therapist. A guide.
- **Tools** – I build rituals. Breathing. Reframing. Movement. Conversations.
- **Recovery** – I rotate. I deflect. I respond instead of react. And I give grace to myself and others.

Just like that ball coming at my head, I flinch, but I rotate.
I adjust. I learn. I *return* to the center. I don't freeze.
I recover the moment with presence.

That is being Unshakeable.

Reflection: The Warrior Within the Reflex

When we talk about being *Unshakeable*, it's easy to imagine that it means we're immune to pain, fear, or reaction.

But here's the truth:

The Unshakeable warrior isn't the one who never flinches, he's the one who trains through the flinch.

That means:

- Owning the inner child who flinches at criticism
- Recognizing trauma without letting it define us
- Staying present enough to *choose* how we respond
- Using our Black Belt Basics not just in sparring—but in silence, stillness, and relationships

If you still flinch... welcome to the human race.
Now let's train for what happens next.

Unshakeable Reminder:

The flinch is not failure. It's feedback. Train through it. Turn with it. Respond with grace. Your scars are not your shame—they are your strength.

"You don't have to erase the flinch.
You just must stay calm enough to finish the move."
- Julien Smith

Chapter 30 - Unshakeable Command Presence

"When the student is ready, the teacher appears.
When the teacher is centered, the whole room shifts."
— Dojo Wisdom / Zen Proverb

There's a Difference Between Demanding Respect and Commanding It

On a hot summer evening, I was driving CJ—one of my young protégés—home from a long day at the dojo. We were tired, sweaty, and hungry. The car was quiet, the kind of quiet that follows a day well spent.

Suddenly, a truck came flying up behind us, veered to the side, and slammed to a stop, pinning us to the curb.

CJ's passenger door lined up exactly with the man's driver-side door. Before we could react, the driver jumped out—and CJ shouted, "He's got a bat!"

Even though I had retired from the force, my training kicked in like muscle memory. I threw open my door, stepped into the chaos, pointed my finger at the man, and barked in a voice that stopped time:

"Drop the bat. Hands on the hood of the car! **Now!**"

He froze. He dropped the weapon.
I had no badge. No uniform. No gun. Just voice, presence, and purpose.

CJ, now wide-eyed, followed my instructions and checked the man's vehicle for other weapons. All clear. I lit into the guy with every ounce of righteous intensity—then took his bat, warned him of what would happen next time, and sent him packing.

Back in the car, CJ broke the silence:
"That was cool, Shihan. But... what were you going to do with your pointed finger?"

We broke out in nervous laughter. The truth was I didn't have a gun, but I did have something valuable in my 'holster': **command presence**.

That incident wasn't about ego or rage. It was about using calm, decisive leadership to de-escalate a dangerous situation.

Command Presence in the Line of Fire

Another time, years earlier, I was backing up a fellow officer who was known for escalating situations. We were called to a bar—bikers, booze, and bad energy. When I arrived, I walked into the nearby parking lot. The officer was nose-to-nose with several angry men, ready to pop.

Then it got worse.

In the shuffle, someone knocked my .357 Magnum out of its holster. It hit the floor, spinning.

For a split second, no one moved.
I knew if I dove for it, it could become a deadly scene.

Instead, I did what warriors do.

In a clear, thunderous voice that cut through the noise, I shouted: **"Everyone stop. Freeze. Don't move."**

And they didn't.

The bikers stood still. Even the officer quieted. I calmly picked up my weapon, holstered it, and then said,
"Backup is on the way. You move, and it's jail for assaulting an officer."

That voice—steady, centered, certain—de-escalated what sheer force never could.

"When the spirit is calm and the purpose is clear,
the room listens—before a word is spoken."
- Simon Sinek

The Ancient Story: The Silent General

There is an old tale of a general in feudal Japan who was both feared and admired—not because of how loudly he shouted, but because of how quietly he led.

In one battle, his army faced overwhelming odds. Morale was low. The younger soldiers begged for a speech, for a rally cry, for something.

The general simply walked the camp, silent and calm, nodding at each man as he passed. He straightened his back, adjusted his sword, and looked each warrior in the eye.

By morning, every soldier was ready to fight to the death.

When asked later why he hadn't spoken, he replied:
"They didn't need more words. They needed my presence."

The Charisma of Stillness

We've all met that person who walks into a room and doesn't suck the air out—but fills it with strength. They don't posture. They don't boast. They simply **are.**

Shoulders back. Chin up. Clear eyes. No drama.
That's command presence.

It's not about having power—it's about being so grounded that others feel safer in your presence.

As a cop, a Hall of Fame Black Belt, and a recovering addict, I've been told many times:
"You don't look like a cop. You don't look like a martial artist. But there's something about you..."

It's not me they're sensing. It's decades of training, surrender, failure, recovery, growth, and spiritual alignment.
It's the Black Belt Basics alive in every breath.

The Unshakeable Core of Presence

True command presence isn't about force—it's about faith.
Faith in our training. Faith in our values.
Faith that we don't need to flex to be felt.

It's walking into a room without fear or apology.
It's staying calm in chaos.

It's knowing exactly who you are—and needing nothing from anyone to prove it.

That's not arrogance.
That's **alignment.**

Building Unshakeable Command Presence

Command presence isn't something you're born with—it's trained into you.

Whether you're walking into a dojo, a boardroom, a recovery meeting, or your own living room after a long day—you carry your presence with you. People feel it before you speak.

Here are a few Black Belt Basics to build that presence:

1. Breathe Before You Speak

One breath can shift the moment. It brings calm, softens reactivity, and gives you control over what comes next.

2. Posture is a Language

Stand tall, shoulders back, chin up—not in arrogance, but awareness. You don't need to strut when you're steady.

3. Speak Less, Say More

A calm, clear voice backed by conviction will always outpower shouting. 'Meaning' carries farther than volume.

4. Lead Without Needing Credit

True leaders don't chase attention. They serve with clarity. They protect what matters. They guide through presence, not pressure.

5. Train When No One is Watching

Presence is earned in private—through discipline, prayer, stillness, sweat, and truth. That's where confidence is born.

Unshakeable Reminder -

You don't have to shout to be heard. Stand still. Breathe deep. Let your training speak louder than fear.

"A true Black Belt doesn't walk in looking for attention.
He walks in already aligned—with discipline in his breath,
purpose in his step, and love in his voice."
- Brad Wenneberg, Shihan

Chapter 31 - When Purpose Becomes Unshakeable

"Fate whispers to the warrior, 'You cannot withstand the storm.' The warrior whispers back, 'I am the storm.'"
- Author Unknown

The night started like any other on patrol—until a quiet call came in that would change everything.

I, along with two other units, was dispatched to a residence in my patrol area. The call came in as a "possible deceased body." That kind of call, sadly, is not uncommon. We responded code two—no lights or sirens, but quick and deliberate.

I was first one on the scene. Nothing looked suspicious from the outside, but I made entry alone, just in case someone inside needed immediate help.

Inside, we found an elderly woman lying peacefully on the bed. After checking for vitals, it was clear—she had passed away some time earlier.

The call had come from her grandson, Joseph. I interviewed him on-site. His story was that he had come to check on her and found her like this. It seemed plausible. No obvious trauma. No forced entry. No signs of struggle.

The coroner arrived, the scene was turned over, and we returned to patrol.

Two days later, homicide called and they told me the truth: the grandmother, 91 years old, had been smothered to death with a pillow.

I was furious.

And I made a vow. I may have just been a patrolman, but I would find out the truth. I wasn't going to let this go. The homicide detectives brought Joseph back in for questioning. Under pressure, he admitted it—he killed her so she wouldn't make noise while he stole her jewelry.

He was booked and locked up.

But the story doesn't end there.

Joseph escaped. He and a buddy of his got out, went back to his grandmother's home, ransacked it, and stole anything of value that they hadn't already taken.

Now I wasn't just angry. I was on a **mission**.

I did what I've done many times before, whether in law enforcement, recovery, or martial arts. I got crystal clear on my **purpose**, built a **vision**, and put together a **plan**.

I began visiting every place Joseph was known to hang out. I introduced myself to his friends and family. I let them know that this man would be brought to justice; and if they were helping him hide, they'd be charged accordingly. I gave them a simple option: turn him in anonymously.

I hit every lead. Every location. Every name I could track.

Still - nothing.

So, I moved to **Phase Two**: legal pressure.

If his crew so much as rolled through a stop sign, they got a citation. Parking illegally? Ticketed. With any infraction—we made sure it was fully legal, fully documented. I had other patrol units on it as well. We weren't harassing; we were applying lawful pressure with discipline and consistency.

The message was clear: we're not going away.

Then… the break came.

A call came in: "He's at the corner store. Right now."

I hit the gas. Tires screeching, heart pounding, I rolled into the alley behind the designated market. A man tried to casually walk away. At first glance, I wasn't sure it was Joseph; but my instincts said, *Check him out.*

As backup units arrived, I approached the man. As I stepped out of the unit, I saw the tattoo - lower left arm. That was him!

He'd changed his look, changed his clothes—but forgot to cover the tattoo.

I unholstered my revolver and approached. He had no weapons. I cuffed him, placed him in the back of my unit, and buckled him in.

Then he looked at me dead in the eye and said the words I'll never forget:

"You don't give up, do you?"

No, Joseph I don't.

He was booked, arraigned, tried, and convicted. He gave up his accomplice.
Both were put in prison - for good.

I wasn't a detective. I didn't have stripes. But I had **purpose**, **vision**, and a **relentless spirit**.

This wasn't just police work, it was Warrior work.

The Warrior's Way

That night on patrol, it wasn't just about catching a criminal—it was about proving, to myself and to others, that relentless clarity and commitment always find a way forward. The same steps I used to bring Joseph to justice can guide anyone facing their own battles.

No matter what your uniform looks like—whether it's a *gi*, a badge, or a name tag—the steps are the same when life calls you to act:

- **Get clear on your Purpose.**
  Clarity removes hesitation. When you know why you're fighting, decisions become simple, and action becomes focused.

- **Create a Vision that guides you.**
  A clear vision becomes your compass. It directs your steps, keeps you aligned with your values, and prevents distraction from knocking you off course.

- **Make a Plan rooted in truth, not emotion.**
  Emotion burns hot but fades fast. A plan anchored in truth

keeps you steady and ensures your actions stand the test of time.

- **Take relentless, ethical Action.**
  Integrity in action doesn't just achieve results - it builds trust, inspires others, and keeps your conscience clear when the storm passes.

- **Don't stop until what's Right prevails.**
  True relentlessness isn't about aggression - it's about refusing to quit until justice, growth, or healing is fully realized.

This story may be from my time on the streets, but the lesson applies anywhere. In your family, your recovery, your business, your dojo—don't quit on what matters. The Unshakeable path is not for the timid. It's for those willing to stay focused, follow through, and fight for something bigger than themselves.

Unshakeable Reminder -

The uniform doesn't define the Warrior—the heart does. Purpose, vision, planning, and relentless action will carry you through any storm. Don't underestimate what can be done with clarity and persistence. A Warrior doesn't give up when it's hard. A Warrior locks in when it matters.

"Evil triumphs when good people do nothing.
When good people stay Unshakeable—justice finds a way."
- Brad Wenneberg, Shihan

Chapter 32 – From Badge to Black Belt

"The call to serve doesn't end when the uniform comes off—it only changes how you answer it."
- Brad Wenneberg, Shihan

The graveyard shift is a strange place to live. The streets are quiet enough to hear your own thoughts — and mine had been getting darker for months.

I was in a tailspin
The pain from my injuries was constant. My nights were fueled by a mix of painkillers, sleeping pills, anxiety meds and alcohol just to keep me upright. I was losing my dream career one shift at a time, and I knew it.

On this night, maybe two months before my medical retirement, I showed up hoping they'd assign me to a desk. I had no partner — just me and the shadows. I told my sergeant I wasn't ready to be on patrol. I told him about the medication, the lingering injuries, the fog I couldn't shake.

He looked at me like he'd heard enough. "You're going 10-8," he said. In service. Alone.

I went through the motions: safety, check; weapons, check; mic, check. On the outside, I was a cop getting ready for another night. Inside, I knew I wasn't fit to be out there. I was a danger — to the public, and to myself.

And that's when desperation came calling. I knew there were no spare patrol cars. So I stepped out of mine, pulled out my nightstick, and smashed the windshield. Over and over. Glass shattered and rained across the hood until nothing was left.

I drove back to the yard. "Sarge, my unit's got a problem," I said, deadpan. "Windshield's gone."

He sent me home. Two months later, I retired.

Losing the Badge

When the badge came off, I didn't just lose a job — I lost an identity. For years, being an officer was who I was. It gave me purpose, direction, and a brotherhood. Without it, I was drifting.

The adrenaline of calls for service was replaced by the quiet ache of not being needed.

Pain can make a man desperate, but loss can make him invisible. I was both.

Finding the Belt

I didn't know it then, but my next uniform would also require discipline, training, and service — just without the badge or the gun. Martial arts wasn't part of my plan; it was a lifeline that showed up when I needed it most.

The first time I stepped into the dojo, I was a white belt again. That was humbling. I'd spent years being the authority, the one people looked to for direction. Now I was a beginner — stumbling through stances, bowing to a teacher, following orders without question.

It was good for me. It broke down what needed breaking and rebuilt me on a better foundation.

Badge and Belt: More Alike Than I Knew

I began to see the connections:

- **Situational Awareness** — knowing where you are, who's around, and what's changing
- **Command Presence** — carrying yourself with calm authority without arrogance
- **Discipline and Training** — drilling until it's second nature
- **Protecting Others** — standing between danger and the people you serve

Both the badge and the belt required courage, but the belt asked something more: humility.

The Samurai Lesson

I once read about an arrogant samurai who sought instruction from a legendary master. The master didn't test his skill — he tested his patience, his respect, his willingness to be corrected.

The samurai failed, because his ego was too big to fit through the dojo door.

I knew that man could have been me; but in the dojo, I learned to listen again. To be teachable. To serve before leading.

A Student's Second Life

Years later, I met a man who reminded me of myself in those early days — a veteran who'd left the service and didn't know who he was anymore. The dojo gave him what it had given me: a new mission. He went from broken to Black Belt, from drifting to directing others. And just like me, he learned that the uniform doesn't define you — the service does.

Unshakeable Tie-In

When I look back now, that smashed windshield wasn't the end of something — it was the first crack of light breaking through.

The badge taught me how to stand for something bigger than myself. The belt taught me how to serve without the armor of a badge. Both were schools of discipline, both demanded sacrifice, and both shaped the man I am today.

Martial arts gave me something the badge never could — a lifelong mission that doesn't depend on age, injury, or title. It gave me a way to keep serving as long as I can bow, speak, and show up.

Unshakeable isn't about never falling — it's about refusing to stay down.
From the graveyard shift to the dojo floor, the call to serve has never left me. It just changed uniforms.

Unshakeable Reminder -

Badge or belt, titles fade.
Service is forever.
That can be our Unshakeable reality.

"Inside of a ring or out, ain't nothing wrong with going down.
It's staying down that's wrong."
- Muhammad Ali

Chapter 33 - A Life Filled with Physical Pain

"Pain is inevitable. Suffering is optional."
— Buddhist Wisdom

People see the uniform, the smile, the power behind the punch or the clarity of my voice—but they rarely see the pain I carry every single day.

I've had more than my fair share of injuries and surgeries. These weren't just random accidents. Many came from years on the streets as a police officer; others from martial arts, high school and adult sports, the wear and tear of a warrior lifestyle, and some from accidents.

Let me give you a sense of it: (not necessarily in order...)

- Migraine headaches
- 4 shoulder surgeries
- 4 foot surgeries (including fusions and a mechanical hinge)
- 7 hand surgeries (including full wrist fusion and partial bone removal)
- A fractured sternum
- A total knee replacement
- Cancer surgery—prostate removal
- And the worst of all: a wrist injury with 3 surgeries and still no clear resolution

That's MANY surgeries and counting.

The Wrist That Won't Heal

This one started differently—slowly. A little swelling. A little discomfort. I figured it was just overuse.

During a routine knee check, my surgeon noticed my wrist and said, "Let's get a quick X-ray."

What we found was shocking.

Two bones in my wrist had completely died and dissolved. Another was close behind. I was diagnosed with a rare bone disease in my wrist with no clear path forward. Even the best in the field didn't know how to treat it.

That process started over three years ago with numerous surgeries, and the pain has not left me.

The Daily Toll of Pain

What most people don't understand is the level of pain this has caused—not just momentarily, but relentlessly. This isn't a "tough it out" kind of pain. It's bone-deep, nerve-sensitive, sleep-stealing pain that whispers at me every moment of every day. My wrist throbs like a war drum. I've forgotten what it feels like to lift a glass without bracing, or to shake a hand without wincing.

There are days the pain radiates through my entire arm, into my neck and shoulder. I must adapt how I dress, how I drive, and how I demonstrate techniques. Pain is part of the rhythm of my day now—and yet I still bow, still teach, still serve. The emotional struggles, depression, fear, anxiety, and sleepless nights add to the misery - body, mind and spirit.

The truth is that I'm not stronger than others, but I've surrendered to a deeper truth. I know this pain is real; but it does not get to be the author of my story.

What Got Me Through

I've needed everything in my warrior arsenal to get through this:

- AA and recovery to keep me spiritually aligned
- Mentorship to stay accountable and humble
- Family and dojo community to remind me I'm still valuable
- Reading and hypnosis to calm my mind
- Mindfulness and prayer to keep me from losing my center
- A sense of purpose which reminds me I still have more to give

And maybe more than anything - a deep, stubborn refusal to let pain define my legacy.

Student Story: The Fighter in the Chair

There's a student at our dojo who came in his late teens. Born with cerebral palsy, he has never walked without assistance. He trains with braces and a wheelchair, but you should see his spirit. He hits pads with fire. He smiles with his whole face. And he bows, as he can, like a warrior.

I once asked him, "What keeps you coming back?"

He said, "This place makes me feel strong. Not sick. Just strong."

That's what this chapter is about. We're all carrying something. The question is—how are we carrying it?

Ancient Story: The Iron Bell

In a small mountain village in ancient China, there was a monk who tended the temple bell.

Every morning at sunrise, he would strike the bell with a mallet—but he had arthritis in both hands. The pain was terrible.

One day, a traveler asked why he didn't let someone else ring it.

The monk smiled and said, "Because pain teaches me to strike with presence, not force. The bell rings deeper now."

I Am Not My Pain

This pain may live in my body, but it will never write my story.

I am a warrior.
I am a servant.
I am a teacher.
I am a man still on fire with purpose.

My wrist may never heal—but I will still bow. I will still lead. I will still pass on every ounce of what I've been given.

Warriors don't walk without scars. They walk with them—boldly.

Unshakeable Reminder -

Pain may limit your motion, but never your meaning. You are more than your injuries. You are Unshakeable.

"You don't become a master because life spared you pain. You become a master because you turned pain into presence—and presence into purpose."
- Lisa Nichols

Chapter 34 - Unshakeable 'Black Belt' Marriage

"A Black Belt marriage isn't built on perfection—
it's built on perseverance, presence, and purpose."
- Quentin Hafner

I met Bonnie on a warm, clear Halloween night. Two of my friends and I were walking home from a party at the mall. I had a pounding headache, and as we crossed the parking lot, we saw two girls walking in the opposite direction. I stopped them and asked if they had any aspirin. One of them—Bonnie—reached into her purse and handed me two.
I like to say that this was the moment I fell in 'lust' with her—and I've had a headache ever since... just kidding!!

She was 15, I was 17, and something beyond the adolescent blitz of hormones sparked between us. It was connection—real and rare.

We only had that one evening together, but it changed everything. Bonnie lived in Southern California. I lived in the north. After that night, we started writing each other daily—actual letters, not texts (texts didn't exist back then!). Eventually, I started driving 400 miles each way, every other weekend, just to see her.

College, track, baseball, it all shortly took a back seat to Bonnie. I packed up and moved south. I had no money, lived out of a van parked near the beach, surfed mornings, worked at a shoe store by day, and spent every possible moment with her.

When we announced our plans to marry—at ages 18 and almost 20—her parents were understandably less than thrilled. We had a motorcycle, no money, and big dreams.

What we also had was *purpose.* From the very beginning, we had a shared vision. We knew what kind of life we wanted to build: one rooted in love, family, joy, service, and freedom. We sacrificed, we planned, and we stayed the course. Bonnie worked to support my dream of becoming a police officer. I will never forget that.

We said we'd wait to have kids until we were stable—and we did. Ten years in, Sheri arrived. Two years later, Jason came along. Our plan—like everything else—was on purpose.

However, life doesn't run on clean outlines and color-coded calendars. We didn't plan for addiction, or cancer, or the valleys that nearly swallowed our whole marriage. There were times we didn't know if we'd make it.

But through it all, there was *us*.

Resilience. Friendship. Acceptance. Faith. Grace. Love. And the stubborn, warrior-like belief that peace was worth fighting for.

When the storms hit, we didn't retreat. We floundered - a lot - and then we built a new blueprint—Black Belt Basics for marriage.

We sought mentorship, counseling, prayer. We rebuilt vision. We created rituals. We cried. We fought. We healed. We loved. And we didn't quit.

What emerged from those battles wasn't just survival, it was *refinement*.

A stronger love. A deeper friendship. A marriage rooted in something unshakeable.

We've traveled the world. Built a family. Raised a village of students. Buried friends and family. Survived setbacks. Held hands through illness. Cried through recovery. And laughed—wow, have we laughed.

Somehow, our success has been grounded in a fierce acceptance of one another… and of the wild, messy, sacred humans we love—even the ones who drive us nuts.

Black Belt Marriage Tools that We Still Use:

- **The 10-Second Rule:** When tension rises, take 10 seconds. Breathe. Delay the reaction. Most "emergencies" aren't.
- **The Duck Test:** If we're having trouble "getting our ducks in a row"… maybe they're not our ducks.
- **The 1–10 Scale:** How important is this—really? On a scale from 1 to 10, is this a hill worth dying on?
- **The Delay Principle:** The greatest remedy for anger is *delay*. Time doesn't heal all wounds, but it sure cools some tempers.
- **The Shared Pause:** When things get foggy, we pause and ask: What are we really fighting for here? Is it 'us' or ego?

- **The "Strip & Redirect" Technique:** When things get too hot to handle... well, redirect the heat. Let laughter (and a little vulnerability) shift the mood. Sometimes a good giggle—and a little surprise—can do more for peace than any argument ever could. (Don't knock it till you try it.)
- **Clarification:** Sometimes one of us just has to ask if what they heard, is what the other one actually said. You might be surprised how often that happens - something very different was heard - so clarification is really valuable.

These aren't gimmicks. They're *practices*—mental and spiritual *kata* that we repeat to keep our marriage strong.

We didn't avoid the storms, and we still can't sometimes. We've learned to bow into them—together.

Unshakeable Reminder:

Love, like martial arts, isn't about perfection. It's about showing up, adjusting our stance, and keeping our vision and values unshakeable.

We are not perfect people - but we're perfectly committed to this life we've built.

That, my friend, is a Black Belt Marriage.

"A Black Belt marriage is built the same way as a Black Belt life—one bow, one breath, and one brave choice at a time."
- Quentin Hafner

Chapter 35 - Experience, Strength, and Hope

"God, grant me the serenity to accept the things I cannot change,
the courage to change the things I can, and
the wisdom to know the difference".
- Reinhold Niebuhr

I've shared much with you—openly and candidly—about my life experiences. I've battled addiction, walked through failures, and made some regrettable choices. I've also discovered strength I didn't know I had; and today, more than anything, I live with a message of hope.

I've been to hell and back, but I never gave up. I never surrendered; and because of that, many of my dreams have come true.

However, I'm not done. I refuse to rest on my laurels. I continue to serve others, grow, and stay right-sized in all I do. I'm far from perfect, but I'm honest, grounded, and at peace. When I rest my head on my pillow at night, I fall asleep without guilt or regret. If I do something wrong, I repair it quickly and own my part.

That's what being a warrior and being unshakeable means: taking responsibility for today, aiming for progress over perfection, choosing purpose, and doing action.

Falling Short, Standing Tall

I am learning from my 'moments'.

Some years back, Bonnie and I went on a cruise along the northeast coast of the United States and Canada. The changing colors of fall were breathtaking. It was one of those rare trips where everything seemed just right. Her parents joined us, and their company was a blessing. Bonnie's mom, Shirley, is full of energy and a sharp wit. Her father, Leo, and I had become true friends. We laughed, explored, and enjoyed each other's company.

Toward the end of the trip, we stayed in New York to attend a family funeral after Shirley's sister passed. Emotions were high, but we were grateful to be present for the family.

Then, on the last day, I had one of those human moments.

At the rental car counter, the employee said something that rubbed me the wrong way. I reacted harshly. Full of anger and self-righteousness, I let my old tapes run the show. I verbally unloaded on her—and embarrassed my family in the process.

It didn't matter whether I was technically right or wrong. I wasn't kind. I wasn't compassionate. I didn't live up to who I strive to be.

I called my sponsor. He listened patiently and then gave it to me straight: "You need to write a letter to the company and make amends."

And I did. Quickly.

He also reminded me: a real apology requires corrective action. It means not repeating the behavior. That's the standard.

Owning our behavior isn't easy. But it's what makes us stronger.

"The ultimate measure of a man is not where he stands in moments of comfort,
but where he stands at times of challenge and controversy."
- Martin Luther King Jr.

The Power of Amends

I gain strength not from appearing perfect, but from learning how to recover from imperfection. I gain hope by walking through failure with humility and emerging wiser. That's what gives life meaning. Unshakeable means I get to choose to recover from my errors - those errors might trip me up, but I get to fix them and move forward.

I cleared away the wreckage of my past so I could live life anew. I let go of resentments—they are death to dreams. When I lived in the past, I forfeited the power of the present. I wasted today.

"Look not mournfully into the past, it comes not back again.
Wisely improve the present, it is thine.
Go forth to meet the shadowy future without fear and with a strong heart."
- Henry Wadsworth Longfellow

Living amends has become a cornerstone of my life. If I yell at Bonnie, saying "sorry" isn't enough. Repeating the behavior invalidates the apology. Real change—living differently—that's what makes it an amends.

My studio—this dojo that I poured my heart into—is my living amends. During my drinking days, I hurt people. I stole. I cheated.

I skipped out on family events or put myself at the center of everything. I wasn't the man I wanted to be. When I got sober, I made a promise: I would build something that served others.

I designed our studio to be a place of healing, growth, and community. Every mat, every lesson, every belt test is part of that promise. I don't just run a business—I run a daily act of repentance and restoration. This place isn't about me. It's about them: our students, their families, and the people we serve.

I live my living amends every single day.

"Your walk talks louder than your talk."
- AA Wisdom

"You can't go back and change the beginning,
but you can start where you are and change the ending."
- C.S. Lewis

Living the Message

When we begin to rebuild, we must also begin to give back. If I don't share the gifts I've been given, they stagnate. I can't keep what I don't give away.

I ask myself regularly:

- What do I have to offer?
- What example am I setting?
- Am I attracting people with purpose?

- Is my life a blessing?

"The meaning of Life is to find your gift.
The purpose of Life is to give it away."
- Pablo Picasso

Each of us has a choice: let our past destroy us—or let it make us stronger.

I made a choice. I chose strength.

Even as a child, I knew I wanted more. I decided the buck would stop with me. I wouldn't be destroyed by addiction, fear, insecurity, or mediocrity. I chose success. I chose freedom. And I still do.

Stories of Strength and Hope

I've seen miracles with my own eyes. In AA, I've witnessed men and women get sober, reunite with their families, rebuild careers, and become the people they were meant to be. But they had to work for it. Nothing changes if nothing changes.

In my karate academy and in my business network, I've seen the same transformations—people doing complete 180s in their lives.

Bethany came to us in 1999. She was broken, defeated, and in an abusive marriage. Her confidence was gone. Her dreams shattered. For months she cried in class and could barely make eye contact. But she never quit.

Eventually, Bethany found her strength. She left that relationship, took custody of her kids, lost fifty pounds, earned her Black Belt, and later became a beloved team member at our academy. Today, she respects herself—and others do too.

Sharon had a similar story. Abused, afraid, and lost, she came to us with two young kids and no hope. But she decided she was tired of being tired. She got to work. She got stronger. She got free.

If they can do it, so can you.

The Way of the Warrior

I will fight the dream stealers. I will not surrender to negativity. I will surround myself with winners and pray for the rest. I will give, serve, and grow.

This isn't just my passion, it's my mission.

Tell me I can't. I'll show you I will.
Tell me it won't work? I'll make it work.
Tell me it's impossible? I'll prove otherwise.

"The chances are that you have already come to believe that happiness is unattainable. But men have attained it. And they have attained it by realizing that happiness does not spring from the procuring of physical or mental pleasure, but from the development of reason and the adjustment of conduct to principles."

- Arnold Bennett

Experience. Strength. Hope.

That's what this chapter is really about.
We all stumble. But warriors rise.
We all get knocked down. But warriors get up.
We all have a past. But warriors choose a future.

You can too.

Let's stop living in the problem and start living in the solution.
Let's be the ones who choose to grow, serve, and lead.
Let's stand strong, palms up, and pass it on.

Unshakeable Reminder -

Every mistake is a chance to grow.
Every scar holds a story of survival.
Experience teaches us, **strength** carries us, and **hope** lights the way forward.
Stay teachable. Stay humble. Stay in the fight.

Our children and students don't just learn what we teach—they become what we model.
They carry forward the messages we embed, often without even knowing it. That's why our work as parents, mentors, and warriors must come from encouragement, not ego... from truth, not just tradition.

I've always been moved by this simple but powerful poem. It captures what many of us feel deep down:

Children Learn What They Live **- By Dorothy Law Nolte**

If children live with criticism,
They learn to condemn.
If children live with hostility,
They learn to fight.
If children live with ridicule,
They learn to be shy.
If children live with shame,
They learn to feel guilty.
If children live with encouragement,
They learn confidence.
If children live with tolerance,
They learn to be patient.
If children live with praise,
They learn to appreciate.
If children live with approval,
They learn to like themselves.
If children live with honesty,
They learn truthfulness.
If children live with security,
They learn to have faith in themselves.
If children live with acceptance and friendship,
They learn to find love in the world.

May we all be the kind of warriors who live in a way worth imitating.
Our real belt rank isn't on our waist—it's in the hearts of those we influence.

Chapter 36 - The Belt You Never Take Off

"When the student is ready, the path appears
- but only if the student is willing to walk it."
- adaptation of the Lao Tzu proverb

There was a time I'd hear the word "change" and react like someone just told me we were out of coffee—panic, denial, and a little dramatic flailing. I'd mutter things like, "I can't handle change," or "I'm just not wired that way." But here's the truth: I was wired that way. We all are. We just weren't trained to embrace it.

The dojo taught me that.

In martial arts, change isn't optional—it's woven into every belt earned, every *kata* learned, every roundhouse kick that starts as a clumsy shuffle. The white belt version of ourselves doesn't get to stay if we want to grow. Every stripe is a surrender. Every belt is a rebirth.

The Dojo Mirror

We tell our students, "The mat doesn't lie." It reflects your conditioning, your preparation, your focus—but it also reflects your willingness to change. If a student isn't improving, we don't hand them a heavier belt and hope it makes them stronger. We go back. We adjust. We fix the foundation.

That's what change is: fixing the foundation.

Sometimes the change is physical—like switching a stance. Sometimes it's mental—like breaking through a limiting belief. And sometimes it's spiritual—like realizing we're not here to conquer life but to serve through it.

I've seen students transform—not just their forms, but their lives—because they were willing to change their approach, their mindset, their story.

Leo's Black Belt Moment (Whether He Knew It or Not)

My father-in-law, Leo, never trained in martial arts—but he absolutely lived the Black Belt mindset. In the early '70s, he was a successful aerospace engineer at Rockwell, working on the Apollo missions. He even helped put the first man on the moon. Brilliant, precise, and methodical. But then came the layoffs.

Leo had a wife, three kids—including my pride Bonnie—and a mortgage. He could have folded. Instead, he pivoted. The man who was anything <u>but</u> a "people person" became an insurance agent. A servant. A provider. A warrior.

He changed. And in doing so, he reframed his purpose.

Leo didn't just change jobs. He changed his life with grace, humility, and quiet courage. That's Black Belt Basics in action.

Alan's Opportunity—and My Resistance

In 1999, one of my Black Belts, Alan, came to me with a business opportunity to share with me. He was excited and on fire with passion.

I wasn't.

I was skeptical. It looked like one of those "networking things." I didn't want to be that guy pestering friends and family. But I also knew something else: as a teacher, my job wasn't to judge—it was to listen.

So, I did.

What I discovered was not what I expected. It wasn't a gimmick. It was a principled business built on mentorship, legacy, and serving others. Sound familiar?

We said yes. That yes brought Bonnie and me more time, more freedom, and more people to serve. But I almost missed it because of my old mindset, the mindset that feared change.

Saying Yes to the Next Belt

Every belt in martial arts represents change. Not just improved skill—but evolved perspective.

A white belt walks in afraid.
A yellow belt starts to believe.
A green belt begins to refine.
A brown belt prepares for leadership.

A Black Belt begins again—with deeper awareness.

That's the secret: every belt is just a new beginning. The belt changes. The lessons improve and grow. The Warrior keeps emerging.

"The highest reward for a person's toil is not what they get for it, but what they become of it."
- John Ruskin

Unshakeable Reminder -

The belts change. The *gi* (uniform) stays the same. We are always students. Change is the mat beneath our feet—it's not something we fear, it's something we stand on.

What's asking to change in your life today—and are you willing to bow in?

"Change is the belt we never take off.
The Warrior doesn't chase comfort—he chases growth."
- Brad Wenneberg, Shihan

Chapter 37 - Culture Is a Decision

"If we don't define our culture, life will define it for us."
- adapted from Carl Jung

In my experience, when we don't take time to build a clearly defined culture (the characteristic features of our everyday existence), life has a way of handing us one we didn't choose. And usually, that one's built on struggle, noise, and confusion.

When Bonnie and I got married, we made a commitment that shaped everything:
We would build our life with intention.

We didn't just talk about what we wanted to do—we talked about who we wanted to be.

We asked the real questions:

- Did we want to stay close to our families or move somewhere new?
- Did we want children right away, or later? How many?
- What kind of energy did we want in our home?
- How would we protect our marriage from negativity, gossip, or outside drama?
- What would our faith life look like as a couple?

We laid it all out. Together.

That became the start of what I now call our family culture. We wrote down our Musts, our Do's, and our Don'ts.

It wasn't about rules. It was about vision. We created a sort of mission statement for our life—something that could help us stay aligned when things got busy or hard.

And yes, we've made plenty of tweaks along the way. Life teaches. We listen. However, the foundation never changed.

We've Done This in All Areas of Life:

- In our marriage: The culture is respect, prayer, laughter, and loyalty.
- In our family: The culture is love, boundaries, and shared meals.
- In our dojo: The culture is honor, humility, and servant leadership.
- In our faith: The culture is grace, accountability, and hope.

We didn't get it all right. But we didn't drift aimlessly either.

We built it. Together.

Culture Isn't a Slogan - It's a Spirit - And an Action

Culture is what lives in the space between decisions. It's the tone. The energy. The example.

It's how we:

- Welcome people

- Correct behavior
- Say goodbye
- Talk about others when they're not in the room
- Show up—especially when we don't feel like it

At the dojo, culture isn't just something we teach.
It's something we live.

When a student bows before stepping on the mat, that's culture.
When a young Black Belt helps a white belt tie their belt, that's culture.
When we clean up the mats after class without being asked, that's culture.

No signs required. The spirit speaks louder.

A Dojo Example

Let me give you a simple example from the dojo.

In a karate class, there are certain non-negotiables—what we call must-nots:

- You must not challenge an instructor.
- You must not act disrespectfully.
- You must not be out of control or disruptive.
- No food or drinks in the training area.
- No everyday shoes on the mat.
- No chewing gum.
- No loud side conversations.

Some may think those are just rules. But they're more than that. They're cultural guardrails.

We don't put them in place to be strict—we put them in place to protect the experience.

Because here's the truth:
If I allow one student to break those standards without correction, the culture begins to erode.

And the breakdown spreads. Quickly.

It's 'monkey see, monkey do'.
What one student gets away with, others notice.
Soon, discipline slips. Respect fades. The sense of purpose that we built that class on starts to fray.

When boundaries are clear—and consistently reinforced—something powerful happens.

The students thrive.

People crave structure, even if they push against it.
They want to know where the lines are. They want to feel safe.
They want to trust that the same principles apply to everyone.

That's the power of a clearly defined culture.

It's not about control—it's about creating an environment where everyone can rise.

"Culture isn't what you say. It's what you do."
- Marc Randolph

Asking for Help

We found that as we worked to build our culture—whether in our marriage, our family, or our business—we didn't always know the next step. Some of our direction, and a lot of our process, came the hard way.

We made mistakes. Took unintended detours. Faced confounding conflicts.

And we realized something:
We needed mentors.
Sometimes, we even needed help from professionals.

We weren't failing, we were growing.

Whether it was a sponsor, a business coach, a spiritual leader, or a wise elder—we reached out.
And it made all the difference.

We didn't let pride keep us stuck. We didn't pretend to have it all figured out.

If the goal was to build something strong, something lasting, something Unshakeable—then whatever needed to be done... had to be done.

No shortcuts. No excuses.

Culture doesn't just come from what we know.
It comes from what we're willing to learn.

The Blessing of Structure

At first, all of this may sound daunting—
Sitting down to define values, writing out musts and don'ts, reaching out for mentorship, making conscious choices about culture...

But I assure you: it's not about perfection.
It's a process.

A process that helped us—repeatedly—along the way.

And more than anything, it gave us one of the greatest gifts of all:
Peace of mind.

When we're clear on who we are, what we value, and how we want to live—we don't waste time in chaos.
We don't lose sleep second-guessing.
We don't let the outside world dictate our inside world.

And that clarity?
It frees up time—real time—to enjoy what matters most:

Time to love.
Time to laugh.
Time to serve.
Time to soak in the blessings that are already in front of us.

Building a culture may take effort at the beginning—
but once it's in motion, it becomes the very thing that sustains us.

Ancient Wisdom: The Garden Within

A young disciple asked his teacher, "Master, how do I create peace and purpose in my life?"

The master walked silently to a small garden, overgrown with weeds. "This is your mind. This is your marriage. This is your dojo," he said.
"If you do not tend to it daily, what grows here will not be what you want."

The student nodded. "So, I must pull the weeds?"

The master smiled. "Yes. And plant what you wish to grow. And guard the gate."

The disciple looked confused. "What gate?"

The master pointed to his own heart.
"The one you leave open when you stop paying attention."

Moral: Culture is a garden. Left untended, weeds take over.
We build it not once, but daily.

"Culture eats strategy for breakfast."
— Peter Drucker

"The way we do anything is the way we do everything."
— Zen Proverb

Unshakeable Reminder -

Culture isn't built in a day. It's built daily.

"Culture isn't what we say -it's what we model, allow, and protect.
It's the quiet current that either lifts people or pulls them under.
And the leader sets the current."
- adapted from Edgar Schein

Chapter 38 - Anger and the Enemy Within

"When there is no enemy within,
the enemies outside cannot hurt you."
— African Proverb

Some people seem to live in a constant state of agitation. Maybe you've met one. Maybe you've been one. Angry without obvious cause. Irritable for no apparent reason. Short-tempered with family, coworkers, even the dog. I know this reality intimately, because I lived it.

And I was sober.

Yes, I was living without alcohol, but I was not living with peace. I barked at my wife. Snapped at my kids. Criticized employees. Grumbled at neighbors. Rolled my eyes at strangers. I was angry, and that anger was poisoning everything good in my life.
It wasn't until Lou, a 93-year-old member of AA, gave me a dose of straight truth that I began to change. I used to pick him up for meetings, and we grew close over time. One evening, after I dropped him off, he came around to my driver's side, leaned in, and said:

"Brad, when you wake up tomorrow morning, look in the mirror and say, 'Good morning, Problem.'"

He wasn't cruel. He was being kind in the most necessary way. He continued, "You're blaming the world for your pain—but the real battle is inside."

That was a wake-up call.

The True Sources of Anger

Anger doesn't always come from a single cause. Sometimes it's like a stew that's been simmering for years. Here are some of the common ingredients:

- Past trauma or feeling like a victim
- Mental health challenges or undiagnosed conditions
- Medical pain or fatigue
- Substance use or withdrawal
- Habitual negativity
- Media influence (TV, talk radio, toxic social content)
- Cultural cynicism
- Emotional/spiritual malnourishment

Often, we're not just angry, we're spiritually unwell, disconnected from truth, love, and clarity.

Resentments and Regrets

Resentment is a form of emotional cancer. Left unchecked, it spreads and consumes. It distorts reality. It poisons relationships. It stunts growth.

- **Regret** keeps us stuck in the past.
- **Shame** makes us feel unworthy of change.
- **Unmet expectations** lead to bitterness.

- **Lying to ourselves** fuels denial.
- **Spiritual crisis** disconnects us from the Source.

The Problem—and the Pattern

I discovered, painfully, that I was easily influenced by others' energy. I mirrored negativity. I let moods and environments dictate my attitude. That realization led me to two small experiments that proved how powerful our influence—positive or negative—can be.

Experiment #1: Creating Sickness from Suggestion

In one of my college-level martial arts classes, I told my staff I was going to run a small social experiment. I picked a student named John. When he arrived, I greeted him warmly and said, "Hey, you doing okay? You look a little pale."

John, full of energy, replied, "I'm great!" But as the class progressed, I had two more students ask him variations of the same question: "You look tired," "You sure you're alright?" By mid-class, we brought him water and told him he looked dehydrated.

John left class early, saying he wasn't feeling well. We debriefed the next day and analyzed it. The point was clear: suggestion shapes belief.

Experiment #2: From Gloom to Gratitude

Each morning, I'd stop at a local convenience store and greet the cashier. He always replied with a defeated tone: "Same thing, different day." His name was Stewart.

I decided to flip the energy. Each morning for five days, I greeted him with enthusiasm: "Hey Stewart! Isn't it a great day?" On day six, before I could speak, he smiled and said, "Hey Brad! I'm having a great day—how about you?"

My energy changed his. Not by force. Not by preaching.
Just by presence.

The Way Through

Anger is a symptom. The root cause is often pain—old, unhealed, denied pain.

The way out? Ownership. Practice. Action. Forgiveness. Surrender.

- Inventory your resentments.
- Make amends—even if the other person doesn't.
- Forgive—not because they deserve it, but because you deserve peace.
- Catch yourself in negativity and reframe.
- Surround yourself with those who uplift, not infect.

Anger thrives in isolation. Healing thrives in connection.

Unshakeable Reminder -

"The enemy wasn't them—it was the fight inside me.
The anger I fed. The pain I ignored. The healing I postponed."
- Lana Del Rey

Chapter 39 - The Heat that Forged Me

"Most people meet their defining moment by accident."
- Author Unknown

When I was a boy, I carried a simple dream in my back pocket.
I wanted to be a protector—one of the good guys.
The kind of man who stood between danger and the innocent.
I imagined heroes who never hesitated, who didn't flinch, who handled fear the way most people handle a handshake.

Like many boys, I mistook confidence for courage and fantasy for preparation.

By the time I was old enough to wear a police uniform, I still couldn't shave without cutting myself. My hands trembled more than I cared to admit.

At age twenty-one, confidence was thin. My understanding of bravery was thinner.
But I put the badge on anyway, hoping it would fill the gap between who I was and who I wanted to be.

It didn't.

Reality doesn't adjust itself to fit our dreams.
Reality is real.
And it has a way of showing up before you're ready.

One night while on patrol fresh out of the academy, at midnight I was dispatched to a residential fire with unknown victims, possibly children involved.

It was the kind of call that tightens a man's chest before he even hits the gas.
When I arrived, the house was fully engulfed. Flames were pouring out of every opening, and injured adults and children were scattered across the street.
Their screams cut through the night with a sharpness I had never heard before.

I was alone.
No backup.
No fire department.
No time.

I rolled up my window, radioed in the severity of the situation, and then stepped out into the heat.
Someone shouted that a boy might still be inside. And in that instant, the boyhood dream collided head-on with the terrifying reality of responsibility.

I ran towards the house looking for any possible entry.
But the windows were exploding outward.
The heat knocked me to the ground.
The air itself felt dangerous.

I circled the structure, desperate for another way in, but every path was sealed by fire.
There was no miracle opening, no heroic moment waiting to happen.
Just danger, impossibility, and a truth I didn't want to face - that there was nothing I could do.

So, I turned back and tended to the injured until help arrived.

When the fire was finally extinguished, we found him, the twelve-year-old boy, on the second floor.
There had been four younger children in the room with him.
He had helped each one out the window to safety.
The last child he physically tossed out, knowing the fall would injure him, but it was the only way to save the boy's life.
Every one of those children survived.

He didn't.

That twelve-year-old showed more courage in his final moments than most grown men show in a lifetime.
He made a life-or-death decision, and he paid the ultimate price for it.

And while he was making the bravest choice of his life, I was outside making a different one.
A necessary one.
A logical one.
A decision that kept me alive — yet haunted me for years.

The Weight Inside

In the middle of the chaos, something inside me broke open. It wasn't panic or paralysis. I never stopped moving. I ran, searched for entry; I pushed into the heat until it threw me back. But inside me, something shifted. It was the weight of realizing that no amount of effort could beat the force of that fire.

Driving home, the feeling didn't fade. It grew. By the time I walked into my apartment at 9:00 a.m., that weight had settled deep inside me. My hands shook uncontrollably.

My heart wouldn't calm. I kept seeing the flames. I kept hearing the screams. I kept replaying the moment I tried to run in and was thrown back by heat. That helplessness became the loudest voice in my head.

And with it, something else slipped quietly out of place. Not just my confidence...
my faith.

I didn't lose belief - I lost connection.
Growing up, I trusted that God watched over moments like these, that if you stepped into danger with a willing heart, heaven would meet you halfway.
But that night, as the flames pushed me back and swallowed that brave boy, it felt as though the line between me and God had gone silent when I needed it most.

It took years to understand this truth:
God hadn't turned away from me - I had turned away from myself.
Shame convinces a man he's been abandoned when really, he's just too wounded to look up.
But at twenty-one, I didn't have that clarity.
I only had the ache... and the distance.

And when a man feels cut off from the One who steadies him, the world gets heavier fast.

So, when I opened that first beer, it wasn't just to quiet the guilt.
It was to fill the silence where my faith used to live.

That single choice lit a fuse that burned through years of my life.
What started to soften the sharp edges of memory became a way to dull everything.

And before long, the fire inside me was more destructive than the one I saw that night.

Unshakeable Reminder -

Here is the part I need others to hear:

If a frightened, shaken, twenty-one-year-old 'kid' too shaky to shave, too overwhelmed to speak up, too lost to fight his own pain, can eventually rise then, anyone can.

That night nearly broke me.
And before anything got better, a whole lot got worse.
But looking back, that was the moment the foundation cracked - the moment that eventually made room for every good thing that would come later.

You don't become unshakeable in the big moments.
You become unshakeable in the quiet ones -
the moments when no one is watching,
and you choose honesty over escape.

A warrior is not unshaken; he is willing.
A warrior does not always win; he always returns.
A warrior faces reality, honors truth, and moves forward even with shaking hands.

"Reality doesn't care about your readiness — only your response."
- Author Unknown

Chapter 40 - The Power of Gratitude – An Unshakeable Basic for Life

"Gratitude unlocks the fullness of life. It turns what we have into enough, and what we dream into possibility."
- Melody Beattie

Gratitude is not a suggestion — it's a strategy. It's not a good bonus on a good day. It's a vital part of living an Unshakeable life.

We train the body, the mind, and the spirit — and gratitude is one of the most powerful disciplines of the spirit. When practiced consistently, gratitude recalibrates our perspective.

It shifts our focus from what's lacking to what's present.
From complaint to contribution. From self-pity to service.

The Spiritual Warrior's Posture

Gratitude is a posture — a way of standing in the world. It doesn't require perfect conditions or perfect balance. In fact, it often shows up strongest when life is anything but perfect.

We express gratitude not because everything is right, but because we choose to see rightly. We give thanks not just when we win, but when we grow — especially when the growth comes through hardship.

For the warrior, gratitude is a steady stance. It keeps our emotions from swinging wildly between victory and defeat. It grounds us when life's punches land harder than expected.

The Antidote to Entitlement

In a world that trains us to want more, faster, and now, gratitude slows us down and centers us. It is the antidote to entitlement, the opposite of cynicism, and the cure for the constant chase of "not enough."

When we live with gratitude, we stop measuring ourselves against others. We start measuring life by meaning. In doing so, we pass on a priceless lesson to the next generation — that life isn't about what we collect, but about what we contribute.

In martial arts, this attitude changes everything. A student who complains about the work will find excuses to quit. A student who practices gratitude sees training as a privilege, not a burden.

"When you love what you have, you have everything you need."
- Author Unknown

Stories from the Mat

I've seen this over the many years in the dojo, and in different forms:

One student, recovering from a car accident, walked in with a limp and a cane. His first words to me weren't about his injury — they were, *"I'm just thankful I can still train at all."* He wasn't blind to the pain. He just refused to let it erase the gift of being on the mat.

Another young student once failed his belt test. Tears rolled down his cheeks as he bowed off the floor. Later that night, he came to me and said, *"Thank you for not passing me — I needed to know I wasn't ready."* That's gratitude in action: seeing the gift inside the disappointment.

Building a Life of Appreciation

Gratitude isn't passive. It's an active force. It shows up in:

- A kind word to someone who's hurting.
- A moment of silence in the morning.
- A handwritten note instead of a text.
- A mental list of blessings, even on a hard day.
- A willingness to say, "Thank you" even when the outcome wasn't what we wanted.

Gratitude practiced daily becomes gratitude lived deeply. We don't have to wait until Thanksgiving. We don't need perfect conditions. We don't even have to feel like it. We simply chose to live it — right here, right now.

When we do, life begins to shift. Our steps become steadier. Our hearts become softer and fuller. Our spirits become stronger.

An Unshakeable Basic for Parents & Leaders

If there's one quality I believe every parent, mentor, and coach should model daily, it's gratitude. It fuels perseverance, fosters humility, and creates the kind of atmosphere where both children and adults can thrive.

When children grow up in a home or dojo where gratitude is spoken, shown, and lived, it becomes the air they breathe. They carry it into school, friendships, and eventually their own families. That's how gratitude becomes part of a legacy.

"Gratitude is the healthiest of all human emotions. The more you express gratitude for what you have, the more likely you will have even more to express gratitude for."
- Zig Ziglar

Unshakeable Reminder -

Gratitude isn't a reaction. It's a decision. One that transforms the ordinary into the sacred, and the difficult into the meaningful.

"Gratitude is the quiet strength of the warrior -
it sharpens the vision, steadies the stance,
and opens the heart to the lesson in every moment."
- Brad Wenneberg, Shihan

Chapter 41 - The Strength of Acceptance

"Acceptance doesn't mean we stop growing.
It means we stop fighting reality."
- Brad Wenneberg, Shihan

There was a time when I thought acceptance was just another word for giving up. It sounded passive, like surrendering to something I didn't want and pretending to be okay with it. But I was wrong. Deeply wrong.

Acceptance is not weak. It's the warrior's <u>strength</u>. It takes far more courage to face what *<u>is</u>* than to keep living in the fantasy of what we wish it were. In fact, most of my suffering has come not from the actual events in my life, but from my resistance to them.

I tried to control everything: other people, outcomes, timelines, even God. I thought if I could just push harder or pray louder, I could make things go my way. But all I did was exhaust myself, frustrate others, and make things worse.

Then came one of the most important lessons of my recovery: *acceptance is not approval*. I didn't have to approve of a diagnosis, a delay, or a disappointment. I didn't have to like it. But I did have to stop arguing with it in order to move forward.

The Acceptance Formula

See it clearly. Accept it honestly. Act with purpose.

Acceptance starts with honesty. Denial is powerful, especially when emotions are involved; but truth-telling is the first act of healing. When I finally admitted I was an alcoholic, it wasn't defeat—it was the beginning of freedom. When I admitted I needed help for bipolar disorder, I wasn't giving up—I was giving in to find the solution.

The same goes for ageing, injury, failure, loss. Every warrior meets these on the path. To accept is to make peace with the battlefield *so you can fight the right enemy*.

Martial Arts and Acceptance

In the dojo, we teach students to flow with movement, not fight against it. When you resist a throw, you get hurt. When you accept the motion, blend with it, and respond wisely, you protect yourself and create opportunity.

Martial arts mirrors life. Whether it's a sparring partner or a spouse, a diagnosis or a disappointment, the principle is the same:

Acceptance creates clarity.
Resistance creates chaos.

Acceptance and Recovery

In recovery, the most quoted words outside of the Big Book of AA may be the Serenity Prayer:

> *"God, grant me the serenity to accept the things I cannot change,*
> *the courage to change the things I can,*
> *and the wisdom to know the difference."*

That prayer is more than a saying. It's a guidepost. It reminds me to stop wasting energy on things I can't fix—like other people's behavior, the past, or the future. Instead, I invest in what I *can* change: my attitude, my effort, my willingness.

My Own Turning Point

I remember a particularly low season in my life. My body was broken from surgeries, my emotions were raw, and I felt abandoned by God. I kept asking, "Why me?" and "When will this be over?" I tried every trick in the book to fix it—until one morning in quiet meditation, I finally said, "Okay. If this is what it is, show me how to walk through it."

Something shifted. I didn't get instant relief. But I did get peace. I wasn't alone anymore, and I wasn't wasting energy on resistance. That moment of acceptance gave me clarity, and with clarity came the next right step.

Unshakeable Reminder -

Acceptance is not the end of action—it's the beginning of *wise* action.

Chapter 42 - Leadership

"A leader is one who knows the way, goes the way, and shows the way."
- John C. Maxwell

At the age of 20 it was my first day in the police academy. There were 34 of us competing for an opportunity to become a police officer. My lifelong dream, my mission — and here I was. I'd passed the written exam, aced the rigors of the agility test, the background exam, lie detector exam, physical, and psychological evaluation.

Wow. The day I'd dreamed about was finally here. I was prepared with my required books, notebook, and pens - all ready to impress everyone with *me* and my so-called super abilities. Class was good and enjoyable.

However, before the day was done, we had physical training out on the field. I was nailing it. After all — *ego* — I had been a champion runner all through high school. I excelled at baseball. So of course, I thought, "I'm going to show them." How arrogant and self-centered I was!

As a group we were running laps around the track. After a few laps our drill instructor yelled out, "Does any of you think you can lap the group?"

Well, well — don't you know who I am! I'm a track star, and I certainly can lap all of these guys. Again... ego. I yelled out, "Yes, Sir! I can do it!" He shouted back, "Then get running."

I broke free from the pack, gained speed, and began to lap the group on the track. When I was about halfway to them again, it dawned on me — I had just broken rank from the team. I knew I'd made a huge mistake. I had allowed my ego to run rampant, and as a result I knew I'd be the first man out.

When I rejoined the group, all I heard was, "You son-of-a... you just showed up all your teammates, you broke rank and tried to prove how awesome you are." The yelling didn't stop there — all the way back into the room for debrief our drill instructor was in my face.

At the end of the briefing, he said, "Mr. Wenneberg, I want to see you in my office right away." Well, Brad — buckle up and put on your big-boy pants, because you're about to be fired on the first day. I was ashamed and wondered what I would tell my wife and friends. I wanted to hide.

I walked into his small office, and he approached me. "You know what you did, right?"

"Yes, Sir. I allowed my ego and immaturity to get the best of me, and I was 100% wrong."

He looked me in the eyes and said, "There are two things I hate: automatic weapons and short cops." (I'm 5'6".)

This is where I learned to be a leader. He said, "Next week you will be the drill instructor. You will lead and manage the group from start to end of the day. If you cannot lead these cadets, you will never be a cop."

I went home that night and, instead of panicking, I made the decision that I would lead with a firm hand — but I would use commands, not demands. I would guide them and hold them accountable. I would not allow anything less than exceptional leadership.

The first day went awesome, and I had things well under control. I went home proud of my leadership performance.

Then along came day three. My drill instructor told me at 3 p.m. to bring the cadet class to attention and then come into his office. He said, "You think you have this group under control and you're being an effective leader?"

"Yes, Sir," I replied.

He had me look through a small peephole into the classroom. There they were — broken from their attention stance, talking and joking around. He said, "That is what I would call a lack of leadership. What are you going to do about this?"

I bolted from his office with a different attitude. I walked with resolve and authority. I understood that leadership started and stopped with me. I needed to set the example and require a culture that worked together — or else there would be negative consequences for those of us wanting to graduate from the academy.

In no uncertain terms, I laid out what was absolutely required of us. They left that night knowing I was their leader, and that there would be no hesitation that I would take action. Not because I demanded it — but because I commanded it.

I got through that week and the next three months that followed. At our graduation party my sergeant (drill instructor) came over to Bonnie and I and said that my leadership skills that I showed that week assured him I would be a great cop.

To this day I preach what goes into making a great leader.

Keys to Effective Leadership

- Lead by example — always.
- Use commands, not demands.
- Hold yourself to the same standard you expect from others.
- Earn respect through consistency, not fear.
- Accept responsibility when things go wrong.
- Build trust by being present and engaged.
- Stay humble — the team comes first.

"Leadership is not about being in charge.
It is about taking care of those in your charge."
- Simon Sinek

Unshakeable Reminder -

Leadership isn't a title — it's a responsibility. It's the courage to set the example, the humility to admit mistakes, and the discipline to keep the standard high.

"A good leader inspires people to have confidence in the leader,
a great leader inspires people to have confidence in themselves."
- Eleanor Roosevelt

Chapter 43 - Six Unshakeable Principles (from the Dojo to Daily Life)

"Teaching is not just a job. It is a human service, and it must be thought of as a mission."

- Ralph Tyler

When we opened the American Martial Arts Academy in 1992, we knew we needed more than a slogan—we needed a compass. Something to guide decisions, to inspire our team, and to remind us of who and how we serve.

Alongside that mission, we set five teaching principles shaped on the mat and forged in real life. Over time, we discovered they were more than class guidelines; they were a blueprint for living... which then became Principle #6.

From Black Belts to Black Belt Living

As the years passed, these principles showed up everywhere—at home, in marriage, in business, in leadership, and in recovery. They reminded us to **catch people doing something right**, to **say 'yes' more than 'no'**, and to **challenge with belief** rather than criticize with shame. Words matter—and <u>how</u> we speak often matters even more.

The world already says:

- "Can't."
- "Not enough."
- "Bad idea."
- "Problem."

We flip the script:

- Problem → Challenge
- No → Growth path
- Correction → Dignity

Examples from the mat and from home

A simple method keeps us aligned: **PCP — Praise, Correct, Praise.** Not fake. Not fluffy. It's respect in action, and truth with a warm tone.

It helps people to maximize their own potential and to help them become the best they can be.

- **On the mat:**
  "Sally, great energy in your strikes today! Next time, let's keep our elbows in to maximize your power—but seriously, terrific job. We're proud of you!"

- **At home:**
  "Thank you for cooking dinner. You're amazing. Maybe just a pinch less salt next time - we loved it, and we appreciate the time you took to make this."

Small shifts change climates.
Trust grows.
Confidence rises.
Culture strengthens.

These are our principles - not just how we instruct, but how we live.

Principle #1 - <u>We Care</u>

- **In the Dojo:**

We care for every student who bows onto the mat—little dragons and seasoned adults alike. We care for families in the lobby, the delivery drivers, and the crew that keeps the floors clean. We listen, notice, serve, and appreciate.

- **In Life:**

Care is a posture, not a program. Brought to the dinner table or the workplace, care says, "You matter." Care opens hearts and builds bridges.

Unshakeable Truth:

Care first, instruct second.

Principle #2 - <u>We Believe</u>

- **In the Dojo:**

We believe every student can earn a Black Belt and grow into a stronger version of themselves—no matter the age, background, or challenge. Belief is our starting stance.

- **In Life:**

Belief in our families, teams, communities - and in ourselves - creates space for courage. Belief doesn't pretend we've arrived; it remembers <u>we're still becoming</u>.

Unshakeable Truth:

Belief is the soil where confidence grows.

Principle #3 - We Challenge

- **In the Dojo:**

We challenge ourselves without shaming. We raise the bar and reach together. Challenge says, "Greatness is in there—let's bring it out."

- **In Life:**

We challenge excuses, stale stories, and comfort zones. Growth requires friction; character is strengthened by resistance.

Unshakeable Truth:

"A smooth sea never made a skilled sailor."
- Swahili proverb

Principle #4 - We Reward

- **In the Dojo:**

We reward progress—belts, stripes, patches, applause, and a sincere word at the right moment. We reward effort, not only excellence.

- **In Life:**

Recognition fuels momentum. A note, a nod, a thank-you, a handshake, a moment of eye contact that says, "We noticed." What gets rewarded gets repeated.

Unshakeable Truth:

Celebrate steps, not just finishes.

Principle #5 - We Praise

- **In the Dojo:**

Praise is specific, sincere, and timely. We highlight courage and effort, reinforce identity, and point to who we are becoming as Warriors-in-training.

- **In Life:**

Praise lifts spirits, eases strain, and strengthens bonds. We speak praise - at home, at work, and in community - because positive identity grows where affirmation is spoken.

Unshakeable Truth:

Catch people doing something right.

"Praise is like sunlight to warm the human spirit;
we cannot flower and grow without it."
- Jess Lair

Principle #6 - We Live It (Within Ourselves)

The first five principles guide how we lead, teach, and love others. This sixth principle holds the rest together. **We live the principles within ourselves.**

"Dare to love yourself as if you were a rainbow
with gold at both ends."
- Aberjhani

Our self-talk becomes our internal instructor. We treat ourselves with the same honor, belief, and encouragement we offer others—because consistency outside requires integrity inside.

1) We Care (for ourselves)
Rest when it's time to rest. Guard peace. Create serenity. Fuel the body well. Kindness in the mirror is stewardship, not self-indulgence.

2) We Believe (in ourselves)
We've fallen and risen. Growth has already happened—and continues. Belief remembers we are a work in progress, with purpose.

3) We Challenge (ourselves)
We hold a higher standard out of love, not shame. We step past the comfort zone and meet the day as Warriors.

4) We Reward (ourselves)
We honor small wins: the sober day, the honest talk, the healthy choice. Self-recognition, rightly placed, fuels gratitude and grit.

5) We Praise (ourselves)
We speak to ourselves as we do to students: specific, sincere, and encouraging. We catch ourselves doing something right.

6) We Live It
From the inside out—on the mat, at home, in our community, and in the quiet places only we can hear—these principles become practice, and practice becomes character.

Final Reflection

These six principles began as teaching tools and grew into a life strategy. They helped us build a school, strengthen marriage, raise a family, nurture friendships, grow a team, and walk the path of recovery with humility and strength.

They are simple, not shallow.
They are steady, not static.

Lived with intention, they shape not only Black Belts - but Black Belt lives - to be Unshakeable.

Unshakeable Reminder -

Care deeply.

Believe boldly.

Challenge bravely.

Reward intentionally.

Praise generously.

Live within.

This is the Unshakeable Way.

Chapter 44 - Listening to the Vibrations Within

"A warrior doesn't just train his body — he strengthens his spirit so he can hear what others cannot."
- Brad Wenneberg, Shihan

Throughout *Unshakeable*, I've made references to faith, spirituality, and moments of what I believe were divine interventions along my journey. Not to preach or convert, but to be honest. After all I've lived through, it would be incomplete to tell my story without acknowledging the invisible force that has guided me across deserts of despair and mountains of triumph.

Spirituality is not one-size-fits-all.
Some pursue it through organized religion. Others feel it in nature, music, meditation, or acts of selfless service. Some search. Some don't. Some believe. Some don't. I don't think there's a "right" answer — only an honest one. It's personal. Sacred. Private.

For me, spirituality has revealed itself as a **vibration**.

Not thunder from the heavens, but a quiet pulsing deep in my soul — a hum I can feel even when I can't hear anything at all. That's my Higher Power's way of guiding me. When I'm lying, cheating, hostile, driven by ego, or disconnected from my purpose, that vibration grows unsettled. I become jittery, uncomfortable — a gentle warning that I am stepping out of alignment.

When I'm honest, humble, kind, and serving others, the vibration softens. It becomes calm... confident... solid beneath my feet. I've learned to trust it — especially in times of darkness.

The "Teacher" Shall Appear

Years ago, after a relapse, I was back in treatment — wounded, ashamed, spiritually bankrupt.

One night I sat alone in a dim room — exhausted, sad, and broken — staring at the floor, praying for strength I didn't feel. Out of nowhere, a nurse appeared. She looked to be in her mid-thirties, radiating peace.

She knelt beside me and asked, "Would you like to say a prayer?"

We held hands across a small table and recited the Lord's Prayer. As we prayed, I broke — sobbing uncontrollably while trying to steady myself with some sliver of hope that recovery was still possible. When I finally opened my eyes... she was gone.

I felt hands then — strong, familiar hands — lightly massaging my shoulders.
It was CJ, one of my dearest friends.

"Where did that nurse go?" I asked, wiping my eyes.

"Shihan," he said softly, "no one else has been in here. I walked in and found you in the dark, crying with your eyes closed. You were the only one here."

To this day I can't explain it.
But I *felt* it — that vibration — steady and certain.

Something greater than myself had stopped by to remind me I wasn't alone.

The Power Within

Our daughter, Sheri, has always been exceptional — she seemed to be born with the heart of a woman already ready for family; but her path to finding the right partner wasn't easy. She had her share of rocky relationships and moments of doubt, wondering if she'd ever find "the guy."

One day in my college class, teaching my students on how to focus on their vision, I called on Sheri and asked her a few simple questions: *What does he look like? How tall? What's his faith? His age? What characteristics do you like the best about him?*

My point was to help her stop drifting and instead get specific — to align her vision with what she truly desired.

Some months later, we attended a wedding together. As we danced, Sheri suddenly began to weep. When I asked what was wrong, she said, "Dad, will I ever find someone and get married?" I told her gently, *"Sheri, stop looking so hard. Trust me — when you let go, he will appear."* That was her message for the night.

Eight months later, she met and then married the man of her dreams. Today, they have three amazing children together.

To me, it was a living lesson in vision and belief — the power of aligning vision with faith, and the grace of letting go.

Staying In Tune

Over the years I've discovered I can't stop the tide of life. I can't control the waves. But I can stay attuned to the vibration within —

because that vibration has never once lied to me. It is how my Higher Power speaks, nudges, comforts, warns, and leads me.

Wherever you encounter your own vibration — protect it. Feed it. Listen to it. Because long after our belts fade and our trophies gather dust... it is **spirit** that makes a warrior unshakeable.

Unshakeable Reminder -

When the world goes quiet... what vibration do I feel within? Am I living in alignment with something greater than myself — or is my spirit asking me to return to center?

"The quieter you become, the more you can hear."
- Ram Dass

Chapter 45 - If They Only Knew

We spend our lives learning to stand tall in the dojo, in the boardroom, in the quiet corners of our homes when no one's watching.
We bow, breathe, and move through the world with poise. People see strength, discipline, control. They see the Black Belt, the leader, the one who always seems to know what to do next.

If they only knew...

If they only knew that even the strongest warriors wake up some mornings feeling like frauds - smiling on the outside while wrestling ghosts on the inside.
That the hardest battles aren't fought under bright lights or in front of cheering crowds; they happen alone, between the ears and behind the ribs.

We polish our image until it shines, then hide behind it.
We tell ourselves lies we've memorized: *I'm fine. I'm strong. I don't need help.*
Lies that keep us looking sharp but hollow us out from the inside.
We forget that honesty, not perfection, is the true mark of mastery.

The older I get, the more I realize this: being "real" is the most demanding *kata* of all.
It's not about how high you can kick or how loud you can yell - it's about having the courage to face your own reflection when the crowd is gone.

Strength without truth is just theater.
And every lie we tell ourselves is another belt we'll never earn.

The Mask of Mastery

People love the image of the master calm, wise, in control.
They bow, they whisper, *"Shihan has it all figured out."*

If only they knew.

Behind the calm exterior, every true martial artist carries a storm. We wear the mask of mastery because the world needs to believe someone's steady at the wheel. But the mask can become heavy - it hides the questions, the fatigue, the quiet doubts that never seem to retire.

Students see certainty; what they don't see is how often I walk into the dojo with my own spirit limping. They see balance, not the fight it takes to stay centered when life tilts hard in every direction.

The truth is, mastery doesn't erase struggle, it sharpens it.
The higher you climb, the thinner the air gets.
And sometimes, the person who seems to have all the answers is the one praying no one notices that he's still searching for them.

We call it discipline, and it is, but it's also armor.
When I tie my belt, it's not always a symbol of victory; sometimes it's a bandage.
It keeps me together when I'm coming apart.
It reminds me: *stand tall, even if the inside is shaking.*

Here's the catch - armor keeps out the blows, and it also keeps out the healing.
Mastery means learning when to remove the mask... to admit that the strongest thing you can do is sometimes to *not pretend.*

Because authenticity isn't weakness - it's the first move toward real strength.

We all wear masks—one for family, one for friends, one for foes, and even one when we're alone."
- Marion Bekoe

The Lies We Tell Ourselves

We all lie - not to others, but to ourselves.
Quietly. Skillfully. Repeatedly.
It's how we survive in a world that rewards polish over honesty.

At work, we say, *"I've got this,"* when deep down we're stretched thin and afraid to drop the ball.
At home, we tell our loved ones, *"I'm fine,"* because admitting exhaustion feels like weakness.
Spiritually, we whisper, *"I'm at peace,"* even when the heart feels like a clenched fist.

The lies aren't malicious, they're defensive.
We build them the way a craftsman builds walls: brick by brick, each one meant to protect.
But protection can become prison.
Sooner or later, the walls we build to hide behind become the same ones we can't break out of.

We tell ourselves, *"I'm supposed to be strong,"* as if strength means silence.
We tell ourselves, *"I'll rest later,"* as if burnout is a badge of honor.
We tell ourselves, *"I'm not enough,"* even when we're giving everything we have.

Here's the hard truth — the lies we tell ourselves don't keep us safe.
They keep us *stuck.*

They rob us of growth, connection, and peace. They keep the inner life - the one that's real and raw - hidden behind a curtain of performance.
And that curtain shows up everywhere:
In boardrooms where leaders pretend they never doubt,
In marriages where partners forget how to be vulnerable,
In spiritual circles where people chase perfection instead of truth.

Every arena - personal, professional, spiritual - has its own costume.
We learn to play the role so well that we forget who's underneath.

However, the only performance worth mastering is the one where the inside matches the outside - where what we show the world is real, not rehearsed.

There's power in truth-telling.
Not the kind that shouts, but the kind that sighs and says, *"This is me today. I'm working on it."*
That kind of honesty changes the air around you.
People breathe easier when someone else finally exhales first.

Compassion Begins Within

We teach discipline, perseverance, and respect but few of us ever learned **compassion for ourselves.**
Somewhere along the way, we decided grace was for others and grit was for us.

We'll forgive a friend's mistakes, comfort a student's fear, and tell our children, *"It's okay. You're doing your best."*
But when we fall short?
The judge inside us never leaves the bench.

We call it accountability, but often it's self-punishment in disguise.
We demand perfection, hide fatigue, and call it leadership.
We confuse suffering with strength, as if bruised spirits earn more honor than healed ones.

In the personal realm, this lack of compassion looks like never resting - always doing, proving, fixing.
In the professional world, it looks like wearing busyness as armor, afraid that slowing down means falling behind.
Spiritually, it shows up as guilt - the endless feeling that no matter how much we pray, serve, or strive, we're still not "enough."

But here's the paradox: **the warrior who cannot forgive himself will never stop fighting ghosts.**

Self-compassion isn't softness - it's strategy.
It's how we break the cycle of inner warfare, how we rebuild trust between the person we are and the person we're becoming.

There's a quiet strength in looking in the mirror and saying, *"You did your best today."*

Not perfectly. Not flawlessly. Just honestly.
Because peace doesn't come when we 'win' - it comes when we finally stop waging war on ourselves.

In sobriety, in marriage, in teaching - I've learned that compassion isn't something you earn after mastery.
It's what allows mastery to happen at all.
Without it, discipline becomes punishment.
With it, discipline becomes devotion.

True strength isn't measured by how much we endure, but by how much of ourselves we're willing to heal.

Being Real: The Lifelong *Kata*

Every warrior has a form they return to, a *kata* that defines them. For some, it's physical; for others, it's inward. The true *kata* isn't about movement, it's about alignment.
It's about bringing the inside and the outside into harmony, breath by breath, choice by choice.

Being real isn't a finish line; it's a lifelong practice.
There's no belt for it. No applause. No certificate.
Just the quiet work of showing up each day and daring to be honest.

In the dojo, that means teaching from truth, not performance.
At home, it means loving without the mask, letting your family see not just the provider, but the person.
At work, it means leading with integrity, even when it costs comfort.

And spiritually it means standing for something greater than ego, and saying, *"I'm still learning."*

Authenticity doesn't demand perfection - it asks for presence.
It's not about having all the answers. It's about living the questions out loud.
The path of mastery isn't about controlling the storm - it's about standing in it and refusing to be anyone but yourself.

So, we keep training.
We keep bowing.
We keep showing up, with fewer masks and more truth.

At the end of the day, being real in body, mind, and spirit is the deepest act of courage there is.

Unshakeable Meditation

If they only knew... they'd see that strength isn't in the stance, but in the surrender.

If they only knew... they'd realize that every warrior bleeds behind their belt, prays behind their pride, and heals behind their humility.

If they only knew... they'd understand that peace doesn't live in perfection - it lives in the space where truth finally meets grace.

So, we bow not to show reverence for what we've conquered, but for what we've survived - and for the courage to keep becoming who we really are.

Reflection

There was a line in a play that sparked this chapter - a wife saying, *"I wish my insides matched my outsides."* and her husband replying, *"I wish my outside matched my insides."*

That moment hit me like a front kick to the chest.
In those two lines lives the struggle of every man and woman trying to find balance between what they show and what they feel.

If this chapter speaks to you, if you've ever worn a mask, ever felt like a fraud, ever battled the distance between your truth and your appearance — then know this: you're not alone.
Every warrior, every believer, every leader, every person walks that same invisible line.

Unshakeable Reminder -

The goal isn't perfection, it's alignment and balance.
To live a life where your bow, your breath, and your being all tell the same story.
To become 'one' with who you are on the inside and the outside.

That's the lifelong *kata*.
That's the fight worth fighting.

"The privilege of a lifetime is to become who you truly are."
- Carl Jung

Chapter 46 - Twelve-Month Unshakeable Challenge- One Month at a Time

"Great minds have purpose, others have wishes."
- Washington Irving

There are some basic principles for success that require daily investment. These involve simple but powerful shifts in routine and thinking—however, the rewards are life-changing. If practiced consistently, these principles begin to work immediately.

The Origin Story

In 1996, I founded and developed the American Martial Arts Academy's Instructor/Business College—a program designed to build leaders in both the dojo and in life. As part of their training, I offered these business and life success principles and challenged the students:

"Do every one of these for just one month."

After thirty days, several of the students excitedly shared:

"Our lives have changed dramatically for the better!"

I was thrilled—and curious.
I asked, "How many of these principles did you actually do every day?"

They replied, "Three, maybe four."

"Wow," I said. "So let me ask you—if doing just three or four made this much impact... imagine where your life would be if you practiced all ten."

They nodded, wide-eyed.
That's when the shift happened.

This is the power of small, daily practices done with intention. One principle alone can move mountains. But practiced together—these create unstoppable momentum.

The Ten Success Principles

1. **Purpose**
   Dreams must stem from your purpose, or the target has no meaning.

2. **Effort**
   There is no substitute for hard work.

   "Opportunity is missed by most people
   because it comes dressed in overalls and looks like work."
   - Thomas Edison

3. **Be Teachable**

   "When the student is ready, the teacher will appear.
   When the teacher is ready, the student will appear."

4. **Mentorship**
   To live a balanced life, each of us should have both a mentor and a mentee.

   "We must be engaged in learning and teaching
   if we are to remain vital."
   - George E. Toles

5. **Reading Program**
   Read at least 15 minutes a day. Focus on inspirational or educational material.

6. **Audio Learning**
   Listen to educational audio every day. Commute time becomes growth time.

7. **Affirmations**
   Use positive self-talk all day. Build good vibrations in your own mind.

8. **Accountability**
   Be accountable to your mission, your plan, your mentors—and most of all, to yourself.

"This above all, to thine own self be true."
- William Shakespeare

9. **Gratitude**
   Focus on your blessings, not your problems. At day's end, take inventory and give thanks.

10. **Workshops & Seminars**
    Attend events for new ideas, support, and staying sharp. Review your notes on these events for continued reminders to stay focused.

Daily Practices to Keep You Grounded

- **Morning Meditation**
  Take a few deep belly breaths. Quiet the noise. Visualize peace, purpose, and connection.

- **Morning Reading**
  Begin the day with a thought, prayer, quote, or passage that lifts your mind.

- **Practice the Success Principles** - as shared above.

- **Evening Inventory**
  Before bed, reflect on the day.
  Any amends to make?
  Anything to be proud of?
  Anything you can do better tomorrow?

- **Responsibility**

"Hold yourself responsible for
a higher standard than anybody expects of you.
Never excuse yourself."
- Henry Ward Beecher

The Unshakeable Challenge

Practice these ten principles every day for the next twelve months. If your life hasn't improved, you can go back to the way it was ... but I doubt you will.

The truth is this:
When we stop investing energy in changing others and instead invest in transforming ourselves, everything changes. The world reflects what we put out.

Live these principles—not for applause, not for perfection, but because it's who we are becoming.

"The fact is, that to do anything in the world worth doing,
we must not stand back shivering and
thinking of the cold and danger,
but jump in and scramble through as well as we can."
- Sydney Smith

"Being teachable is a high form of spirituality,
but remaining teachable is the highest."
- Kate L. Kirkham

Chapter 47 - Pass the Torch - The Final Challenge

"Don't die with your music still in you."
- Dr. Wayne Dyer

It's been said that the richest place on earth is the graveyard.

Why?
Because buried there are unwritten books, unsung songs, unspoken apologies, unlived dreams, unstated businesses, unreleased resentments, and undeclared love.

Too many people take their gifts, wisdom, creativity, and potential to the grave - never shared, never fulfilled, never passed on.

But not us.
Not the Unshakeable Warriors.
Not on our watch.

We don't hoard wisdom. We share it.
We don't wait for perfect. We act.
We don't just learn. We teach.
We don't cling to the torch. We pass it.

Legacy, Family, and Gratitude

When I opened our dojo in 1992, it was never a solo act. From day one, it was a team effort led by my wife Bonnie, our children Sheri and Jason, and my in-laws, Leo and Shirley. Together, we stepped onto the mat of possibility with full hearts and zero doubt - we <u>were</u> going to build something special.

And we did.

Jason has taken the reins of operations, staff development, and finances with wisdom and strength. Bonnie and Sheri built an incredible after-school karate program that has positively shaped the lives of countless children. And Leo and Shirley's steady love and support have been the rock upon which we all stood.

Watching my wife and children each earn their Black Belts - and grow into remarkable leaders and entrepreneurs - has brought more joy to my heart than any trophy ever could.

What began as my dream has become our legacy, and I am more grateful than words can express.

The Final Challenge

This chapter isn't about legacy in a big, grandiose way. It's not about fame, or buildings with your name on them. It's about something deeper. It's about having the courage to live full and die empty.

What will people remember you for?
What impact will outlive you?
What seeds are you planting that will grow long after you're gone?

This is the final challenge - not to finish first, but to *finish fulfilled.*

Don't Rob the World of Your Song

Somewhere inside, you know there's more in you. A story. A message. A lesson. A song. A smile. A blessing.
It's not too late.

Whether you're 6 or 96+ (as of this writing, my mother-in-law is 96 and still laughing!), you still have something to give. If you're breathing, you're not done yet.

I wasted years stuck in fear, addiction, ego, and confusion. I almost took my life - and my purpose - with me. But by God's grace, I stayed - I healed, I shared, and now, I serve.

Every time I bow into the dojo, I remind myself: this could be the last class.
Make it count.
Every time I speak or write or teach, I ask: did I give them my heart?

If the music in you is still playing - sing.
If the lesson is still unshared - teach.
If the torch is still in your hand - *pass it.*

Unshakeable Reminder -

"I want to be thoroughly used up when I die, for the harder I work, the more I live. I rejoice in life for its own sake. Life is no 'brief candle' to me. It is sort of a splendid torch which I have a hold of for the moment, and I want to make it burn as brightly as possible before handing it over to future generations".

- George Bernard Shaw

Chapter 48 - After the Final Bow

"It's not how you start - it's how you bow out."

There's something sacred about that final bow at the end of class.

For the students, it may feel like just a routine — feet together, hands by the sides, bow to the instructor. But for me, it's always been more than that. It's a moment of gratitude, of humility, of respect for the time we shared, the work we put in, and the chance to do it again tomorrow.

Note from the Mat

This isn't a farewell. I'm still here, still teaching, still bowing in and out of class every day. But this chapter is about legacy—about living in a way that, when the final bow does come, it means something.

One day, though, there won't be tomorrow.

One day, the mat will go quiet, the *gi* will hang for the last time, and I'll take my final bow. That's not a sad thought. It's a motivating one because how I leave the mat - and this life - matters.

When the students gather, and the dojo continues without me, what will they remember?

Will it be the perfect punch? The sharpest *kata*? Probably not.
They'll remember how I made them feel.
They'll remember if I showed up for them.

They'll remember the laughs we shared, the tears we shed, and the hard lessons we pushed through together.

They'll remember if I lived what I taught.

I used to think legacy was about accomplishments - trophies, rank, recognition.

Now I know it's not about being remembered for what I did —
It's about helping others become who they were meant to be.

My life has been full of second chances. Grace. Recovery. Discipline. Family.
I've learned to live with my palms up, to give more than I take, and to always leave the mat better than I found it.

And I hope that when I take my final bow, someone else will be inspired to stand up, tie their belt, and begin.

That's all I've ever wanted.

Not applause.
Just impact.

What's the Legacy

Sometimes I wonder what the students will say about me when I'm gone.
Not on the day of my last class — but years later, when they're tucking in their own kids, or standing tall at a podium, or fighting through a dark night.

Will they say I was tough? Probably.
Will they say I taught good karate? Maybe.

But what I really hope is...
They'll say I showed up.
Showed up with my whole heart.
Showed up when it was hard.
Showed up for *them.*

That's what mattered most to me. Not how straight their punches were — but how strong their spirit became.

I wanted to be more than a *Shihan*. I wanted to be a steady hand when life got shaky. A firm voice when fear got loud. A mirror that helped them see the warrior already inside.

If they remember anything about me, I hope it's that I *saw them.* Really saw them. Not just their rank or potential — but their pain, their hope, their grit. I hope they remember the times I believed in them when they didn't believe in themselves.

Because I remember the ones who believed in me.

That's why I kept showing up.
Even when I was tired. Even when I was broken. Even when the voices in my head told me I had nothing left to give.

I showed up anyway. Because that's what warriors do. In the end, if that's what I'm remembered for — that I kept showing up — that's enough.

But life doesn't stay the same, does it?

"The two most important days in your life are
the day you are born and the day you find out why."
– Mark Twain

There's a reason we bow *in* and we bow *out.* Everything has its season — including me.

As the years went on, I noticed my punches weren't as fast, my kicks not as high. My body, once forged like a weapon, started whispering things I didn't want to hear.

The injuries came like uninvited guests:
Knee replacement.
Shoulder surgeries.
Cancer surgery.
Then the rare bone disease — the one that's led to multiple surgeries on my hand... and still no guarantee of normal function.

Each one taught me something. Each one humbled me. Each one became part of my training — not on the mat, but in my spirit. I've fought these battles like a warrior, not always winning, but always rising.

Eventually, I had to accept that the studio no longer needed me the way it once did. My son Jason stepped in, taking the reins with strength and confidence that I had always hoped he'd grow into. Alongside his crew, he made sure the dojo would not only survive — but thrive.

And while I was proud... I also struggled.

There were moments when I felt like a guest in my own creation. Like a statue in the back corner — respected, but no longer central.

I didn't know what to do with that at first.

I had built this place out of my pain and redemption. It was my living amends — my gift to the community, to the kids, to the person I had once been. And now, it didn't *need* me.

That's when I learned the next great lesson:
Legacy is letting go with grace.
It's trusting that what you built was strong enough to stand — even without you holding it up.

It doesn't mean you're not important.
It just means your role has changed.

And with time — and a little humility — I understood in my heart that I *was* still needed. I still mattered. I still had something unique to offer.

It just looks different now.

I shifted my focus. I began teaching only the advanced students — the teens, the adults, and especially our Black Belts. These were the ones deep in the journey, where my decades of experience, my battle scars, and my quiet wisdom could be most valuable.

I began to write my first book, *Unleash Your Inner Warrior*. That writing became a form of healing, of storytelling, of sharing my experience, strength, and hope with others far beyond the dojo walls.

I eventually found myself consulting to martial arts studios around the world — helping other instructors create cultures of excellence, integrity, and heart.

I also became a motivational speaker, stepping onto new stages — not just mats. I told my story. I shared the stumbles, the scars, the victories, and the recoveries. I spoke to students, parents, CEOs, recovering alcoholics, and everyone in between. The message was always the same:

You are not done.
You are never too far gone, never too broken, and never too old to serve.

Somewhere along the way, I even dusted off my old love of magic - a childhood fascination that turned into a way to make people smile again. It was playful. Light-hearted.

A reminder that joy is a tool also — one we all need in our belts.

Through all of this, I had to adapt. Reinvent. Shift from being the main act to the steady guide, the backstage hand, the storyteller by the campfire.

My Black belt — once crisp and new — is now worn, soft, and nearly turned white again from decades of use. The color has faded, but the commitment hasn't.

At 72 years old, I'm still in the game.
Still training.
Still learning.
Still giving.

And one day, when I tie that belt for the last time… I'll know I didn't just wear it.
I loved it.

To My Family, and the Next Generation of Warriors

To my Black Belt wife Bonnie, our kids Sheri and Jason, their beloved spouses (ALL committed Black Belts), our grandkids, and the students who have become family...

This journey — this dojo, this life, this legacy — was never just about me. It was always about *us.*

I may have been the founder, but you are the future.

I've watched you rise, stumble, grow, and lead. I've seen you carry the mission forward with strength, grace, and your own unique wisdom. You've taken what I built and made it better — more alive, more relevant, more powerful than I ever could have imagined.

To Jason — thank you for stepping in, stepping up, and carrying the flame. I see the love you pour into the students. I see the excellence you expect, and the heart behind your leadership. We've shared a secret handshake since you were just a kid — a simple but sacred connection that only we understand. That handshake still means everything to me. I am proud of the man you've become — as a son, a father, a leader, and a true quiet warrior in your own right.

To Sheri — the apple of my eye. We've always had a special bond - one I can't fully explain but deeply treasure. You've been my sounding board, my heartstring, and my steady light. Your strength is quiet but fierce. You have always reminded me of what matters most, and I carry your love with me in every decision I make. I am so proud of the woman you are - wife, mother, protector of all - you are a true warrior.

To Jorge and Crystal — thank you for locking your arms with our family and giving your best to the cause. You're not just supporting the mission — you're living it. The way you love, serve, and show up is a testimony. You've taken on the weight of the vision and helped carry it forward with excellence and humility. I'm so proud of you both, and I love you as if you were my own.

To our grandchildren — I hope you know that every bow I took, every lesson I taught, every tear I wiped, and belt I tied... it was also for you. A path being laid, one step at a time, so you'd know what's possible when you live with integrity, courage, and open hands.

And to my wife Bonnie — my partner, my love, my greatest support... you've walked beside me through every storm and every celebration. You believed in me when I didn't. You stood behind the scenes while I stood out front. Without your quiet strength, none of this would have happened. This life we've built — and the legacy we leave — belongs to you too.

You'll always be my Frog. I'll always be your Eagle.
No matter what, our lucky number - (smile...) - will always be ours. A reminder that even when life made no sense... we had each other, and always will.

An Extra Note to My Family

As I reflect on the legacy we've built through this academy, I want something to be crystal clear, especially to my children and grandchildren:

You are not bound to this business.
You're not expected to follow in my footsteps.
This academy is *my* living amends, *my* purpose, *my* service.

This legacy isn't about the building or the academy.
It's about "becoming".
And I trust your hearts to lead you wherever you're meant to serve.

If you choose to carry it forward, I'll be honored. If your path leads elsewhere - to new dreams, new passions, or far-off destinations - you have my full and unwavering support.

This place was built out of love, not obligation. Let your own calling guide you. And wherever that calling takes you... I'll be in the front row, cheering you on.

To Be Clear

This isn't a goodbye. I'm still here — in body, mind, and spirit.
I'm still training, still teaching, still speaking, still *serving.*
This isn't the last bow — it's just a moment to look around and appreciate the journey.

I may move slower. I may teach differently. I may lean more on wisdom than speed.
But, make no mistake — I'm *still in the fight.*

Before I go, let me say the words I've spoken after thousands of classes and events — words that carry our mission, our heart, and our humor:

"We did it again."

We served.

We laughed.

We loved.

We grew.

And to my family —

"I love you more than a thousand banana splits."

"What you leave as a legacy is not what is
etched in stone monuments,
but what is woven into the lives of others"
– Pericles

Unshakeable Reminder -

You're not done until the final bow — and I'm not even close. I'll be here, palms up, belt tied, loving every minute until that final day does come.

Chapter 49 - To My Unshakeable Readers

I've poured my blood, sweat, and tears into this book.

Unshakeable - To Live a Life with Strength, Focus, and Heart
isn't just a collection of stories - it's my life. The wins, the failures, the laughs, and the pain. I wrote every chapter with one hope in mind:

That something on these pages will make a positive difference in <u>your</u> life.

Maybe it's a story that sounds familiar.
Maybe it's a line that echoes something you've been feeling.
Maybe it's just the reminder that you're not alone.

Whether you're happy and thriving, or hurting and barely hanging on—I believe something in this book will resonate with you. These lessons aren't just martial arts principles. They're life principles. They're *survival* principles.

There was a time I was lost. Hopeless. Slowly committing spiritual suicide.
But through surrender, faith, recovery, and some old-school Black Belt basics, I found a way back.

And if I can—*so, can you.*

Unshakeable Defined

To be **Unshakeable** doesn't mean we'll never be shaken.
We <u>will be</u> — by loss, by fear, by failure, by life itself.

But it's not the shaking that defines us — it's how we *respond* to it.

To live Unshakeable is to rise when the world tells you to surrender.
It's to breathe through the storm, steady your stance, stand tall in the rain, and find grace in the grit.
It's the quiet strength that gets you out of bed when your heart is heavy.
It's the voice that whispers, "Keep going," when everything inside you wants to stop.

Unshakeable is humility wrapped in courage, and faith refined through fire.
It's the choice to keep showing up — disciplined, compassionate, and true — no matter what tries to knock you down.
It's not perfection. It's presence. It's perseverance. It's purpose.

Being Unshakeable isn't about avoiding life's blows —
it's about *absorbing them, learning from them, and still standing tall.*

That's the way of the Warrior.
That's the way of the Heart.
That's **Unshakeable.**

Thank you for taking the time to read this.
It means more than you'll ever know.

"The Warrior's greatest victory is not over others,
but over the self—every single day."
- Brad Wenneberg, Shihan

Unshakeable Reminder -

"Infuse your life with action.
Don't wait for it to happen.
Make it happen.
Make your own future.
Make your own hope.
Make your own love.
And whatever your beliefs, honor your creator,
not by passively waiting for grace to come down from on high,
but by doing what you can to make grace happen yourself,
right now,
right down here on Earth."
- Bradley Whitford

With deep respect and gratitude,

Brad C. Wenneberg

Husband, Father, Grandfather, Shihan, Warrior in Progress

Acknowledgments

A warrior may stand alone in the arena - but no warrior *ever* gets there alone. *Unshakeable* was forged the same way a Black Belt is earned - through the loving correction, guidance, encouragement, laughter, and sacrifice of many people who believe in the mission.

To Bonnie, my Frog. You've been with me through every bow, belt, bruise, and broken bone — and you still haven't kicked me out of the dojo (or the house). For more than fifty years, you've been my partner in life, love, and every crazy adventure I've dragged you into. From late-night belt tests to endless karate stories, you've heard it all and supported it all. Thank you for being my anchor, my laughter, my partner, my encourager, my truth-teller, my safe place, and my Love. You have stood by me in every season — through hardship, healing, addiction, recovery, and the building of a life and legacy together. Eagle & Frog Forever!

To my children, Sheri and Jason, their spouses Jorge and Crystal, and the family who surrounds us - thank you for your love, patience, and faith through every season of this journey. Your unwavering support of your 'old man', your terrific ideas that have propelled my dreams forward, and your creativity and assistance in even the everyday parts of AMAA, fill my world with joy and blessings.

To my father-in-law (z'l) and mother-in-law (z'l - sadly, she passed just before this publishing), Leo & Shirley Cohen - a very special thank you because you believed in my Vision, Dream, and

Purpose, and inspired me to "Go for it!" from the very beginning. You have been true blessings and a great part of this legacy.

To 'Shihan's Posse' - the adults who help carry the torch at American Martial Arts Academy - you are the quiet but strong force behind the scenes that makes AMAA what it is. Special thanks to Tom Barbarick, Marty Holt, David Goo, Deidre King, Carlo Quintana, and Adrian Corfar.

To every instructor, parent, and volunteer whose passion gives our students an *Unshakeable* experience, and To your families and spouses - thank you for your willingness to share your time and your warrior with this dojo and its mission.

To my lifelong friends, students, and "other kids" - Nikhil and Megan Joshi, and Caleb Beller and family - thank you for walking beside me, trusting me, and believing in this Unshakeable message as much as I do. You are more than students, more than Black Belts - you are family.

To the fellowship of Alcoholics Anonymous and Al-Anon - you taught me how to get honest, stay humble, laugh at myself, and live life one day at a time.

To Jack C., Al v.T., Jerry H., Ed C., Chuck J., Richard E., Joe R., Corey M., Rick, Danny B., and so many others - your friendship, mentorship, tough love, and outrageous sense of humor kept me alive long enough to become the man and husband I was always meant to be.

To my Karate Teachers - I met my first instructors in 1986, at a time when I was still recovering from the wreckage of my addictions. Dan Ahrens, Sensei, was my first teacher in Goju-Kenkyu. He helped put my broken body back together, piece by piece. Dan remains one of the finest martial artists I've ever seen, and it wasn't just his skill that impacted me - it was his faith in my recovery. When I was still fragile, he believed in me. That belief gave me the hope I needed to keep moving forward.
I began training with Bob Gray, Shihan, in 1993, and he has been my Master Instructor ever since. He is one of the most gifted teachers I have ever encountered. More than that, he has been my mentor, my friend, and my spiritual guide. He has seen me in the darkest valleys and in the brightest moments, and through it all, he has never left my side.
For over four decades, these men have molded, trained, and believed in me. Their influence is woven into everything I teach, every class I lead, and every word I write.
I am forever grateful.

To every editor, reader, friend, mentor, and truth-teller who challenged me, pushed me, and reminded me to keep this raw and real - thank you for helping me bring this *Unshakeable* message to life.

Finally, to my Higher Power whom I choose to call God - Thank You for second chances, for daily grace, and for the opportunity to be of service. May every page of this book point back to where my strength truly comes from.

Brad C. Wenneberg was born and raised primarily in Southern California, with formative years also spent in Northern California, where he graduated from high school. He later attended Golden West College and Fullerton College, earning an Associate of Arts degree in Police Science. In 1973, Brad graduated from the Fullerton College Police Academy and served as a patrol officer with the Anaheim Police Department until 1978.

Following a medical retirement from law enforcement, Brad transitioned into the insurance industry, where he worked as a broker for twelve years. During that time, he distinguished himself as a top producer, earning membership in the prestigious Million Dollar Round Table.

In 1992, Brad founded the American Martial Arts Academy (AMAA) in Fullerton, California. What began as a small single karate school has grown into a 15,000-square-foot, multi-million-dollar Academy serving more than 1,000 students at its primary location, with a sister school serving over 500 additional students. Over the past three decades, AMAA has empowered thousands of children, teens, and adults to build confidence, discipline, and character.

Brad serves as Shihan and Master Instructor of AMAA and is co-owner of the Academy alongside his wife, Bonnie, to whom he has been married since 1973. Together, they are also co-founders of MA Business and Consulting University, an organization dedicated to mentoring, training, and developing business owners and leaders.

Family is central to Brad's (and Bonnie's) life and work. Their two adult children, Sheri and Jason, along with their spouses, work alongside Brad and Bonnie in the Academy and also other related ventures. Sheri and her husband, Jorge, are the parents of three amazing and wonderful children. Jason and his wife, Crystal, have two amazing and wonderful children. As a family, they share a deep love for training, traveling, and time together.

Outside the dojo, Brad is a lifelong student of magic and astronomy and a devoted writer, interests that reflect his enduring curiosity, sense of wonder, and passion for teaching. His work - both on and off the dojo mat - centers on service, integrity, discipline, and helping others discover and maximize their own potential.

www.ingramcontent.com/pod-product-compliance
Lightning Source LLC
LaVergne TN
LVHW091020080826
845145LV00002B/309

* 9 7 8 1 9 6 9 8 2 6 2 4 5 *